The Kindergarten Teacher's Very Own Student Observation & Assessment Guide

by
Judy Keshner

MODERN LEARNING PRESS
ROSEMONT, NJ

Acknowledgement

Special thanks and appreciation to Robert Low,
who saw the merit of my work and
how to organize it to benefit others.
His vision and patience enabled this book
to become a reality.

ISBN 1-56762-061-2
Copyright © 1995 by Judy Keshner

Dedication
This book is dedicated to my friend,
master teacher Cathy Busby,
who understands the magic of childhood,

and to Tyler, Casey, and Danni,
my grandchildren,
who are living it.

Contents

Introduction

Assessing today's kindergarten children is an ongoing process that begins when the teacher and child first meet, and ends when the child moves on to a new teacher and classroom. Rather than relying solely on formal test instruments, which attempt to measure children performing tasks in an artificial way, early childhood educators increasingly recognize the importance and validity of observing children's activities in the classroom, documenting them in an organized format, and assessing them in relation to the range of expected "outcomes" for children in this particular grade.

Information compiled in this way provides educators and parents with a crucial perspective on the development of kindergarten students, and it serves as the basis for effective instruction during the kindergarten year. Because kindergarten teachers preside over children's first real school year, we have a special responsibility and opportunity to help identify those who have unique needs and/or special talents, to chronicle the remarkable progress most children make during this important year, and to provide parents with an evaluation of their child that is likely to have them nodding their heads in agreement.

Most of all, however, we need to gather accurate information about each child's individual capacities and needs for our own "primary" purposes — to teach each child to the best of our ability, and to help each child make a successful transition into the school system.

Experienced teachers know that the process of observing, documenting and assessing children's activities can be difficult and time-consuming. Even with a small number of students, an aide, and supportive parent volunteers, the many needs and demands of kindergarten children rarely allow time for sustained observation and evaluation during school hours. And, now that increasing numbers of kindergarten teachers are coping with large class sizes, a lack of support personnel, indifferent or hostile parents, and a wide range of children (many of whom are coping with serious and complex problems of their own), gathering the needed information and organizing it in an effective format may seem virtually impossible.

These sorts of pressures are what led me to start developing the assessment forms and overall system described in this Guide. During my 28 years as a kindergarten teacher, I progressed from writing a limited number of notes on index cards to creating assessment sheets linked to specific aspects of the curriculum or of a child's development. These sheets were all designed to be filled out right in the midst of the school day, when the children are actually being observed. This not only allows teachers to compile the most accurate information, it minimizes the amount of "extra" time needed for the assessment process.

These sheets will enable you to record your observations of each child — and the group as a whole — in an acceptable and accountable way, without the burden of having to fill out overly complex checklists and lengthy reports. I designed the sheets to be easy-to-complete and easy-to-read, yet full of pertinent information that creates a clear picture of each student. All the sheets are clearly labeled as to the area being assessed — such as social development or learning centers. Both strengths and weaknesses in these areas can be easily identified, and growth in each area is visible over time.

More information about the kindergarten assessment process and the assessment sheets I developed appears in Chapter 1 of this Guide. You'll then find an overview of the schedule for using the assessment sheets, and suggestions for using them. This section is followed by a series of chapters which explain in detail the areas being assessed, the information compiled by specific sheets, how to compile the information, and how to utilize it. After a brief conclusion, you'll also find a list of Recommended Resources which I and many other kindergarten teachers have found helpful.

I hope this Guide and the accompanying materials will both enhance and simplify the process of assessing your students. As you become more comfortable and experienced recording your observations, you will find the process less time-consuming and more automatic. You may even, in fact, find it a particularly interesting and satisfying part of the daily routine. After almost three full decades of kindergarten teaching experience, I am still amazed and intrigued by all I learn from "my" children. And, the better I get to know them, the more rewarding the school year is.

...you will find the process less time-consuming and more automatic.

Teaching can and should be a constant learning experience — an adventure that natural assessment helps to organize and facilitate. The materials I developed help me do my job better and enjoy the experience more. I hope and believe they will do the same for you.

Assessing Kindergarten Students – An Overview

What are the "baseline" abilities of the children entering kindergarten?
What are their current developmental levels in the social, emotional,
physical, and intellectual realms?
Do any show signs of having special needs?
How are they responding to their school work and their classmates?
What sort of growth and development are they demonstrating over time?
How can I best teach each one, as well as all of them together?

Kindergarten teachers start each year with many questions. Unlike teachers in the following grades, who have the luxury of reviewing records from one or more previous years of school, we kindergarten teachers must act like scouts in an unexplored territory, finding our own way and leaving accurate signposts for those who will follow us. And, in so many schools, the obstacles we face along the way seem to increase with each passing year.

Finding answers to our questions has always been difficult, but it has become especially difficult with today's kindergarten students, who are far different than the children I first began working with in the late 1950's. The changes in our families, communities, and entire society have had a tremendous impact on young children, and in many cases the "condition of the kids" has grown worse instead of better.

A number of the problems that now seem "routine" were either unrecognized or virtually nonexistent just a few decades ago. And, there has also been a noticeable increase in the sheer diversity of the student population. Different backgrounds, different lifestyles, different age levels, different capabilities — all converge in the kindergarten classroom and make the job of the kindergarten teacher more complex than it has been in the past.

This new complexity increases the need for accurate assessment of individual students, yet it also leaves us less time available to do the observation and record-keeping that are essential parts of our job. To further complicate matters, the instructional methods and materials used in most kindergarten classrooms have also changed markedly over the last decade or two, creating an even greater need for new assessment methods and materials.

These sorts of pressures are what led me to develop and compile the assessment forms and techniques described in this book. Over the years, I had learned what type of information I needed to do my job well; the difficult part was figuring out how and when to compile it. Eventually, I started creating some checklists which met my own needs as a (hard) working kindergarten teacher, and I soon found I could fill them out right in the classroom during school hours. I then began refining the checklists, adding new ones as needed, and further developed the techniques that enabled me to observe and record right in the midst of the daily activities — the most efficient and accurate way to assess. The information and materials you now have are the end result of this learning-by-doing process.

What to assess, and why?

Early childhood professionals have traditionally observed and organized information about such student traits as:

> behavior patterns,
> dispositions,
> interactions with other children,
> ability to handle materials,
> physical growth and coordination,
> levels of cognitive awareness and skills,
> developmental milestones,
> use and understanding of language.

This sort of information helps us understand the unique strengths and needs of the children in our classes, which in turn helps us determine how best to teach each individual student. To compile this sort of information, we collect children's work over time and observe the growth shown. We keep anecdotal records of incidents and behavior. We jot down notes about kindness shown or aggressive acts. We check the progress demonstrated when children attempt or complete simple tasks, and we watch children interacting with materials and each other. We then need to organize all this information in a way that makes it easy to understand and to use.

This Guide and the materials in it are designed to help you record and organize the daily, weekly, and monthly observational data that you gather during the school year. Rather than relying on memory or unorganized notes, the enclosed assessment forms facilitate systematic and sequential recording of the growth of each child — and the class as a whole. These materials cover specific areas and lessons throughout the kindergarten year, showing physical, emotional, social, and cognitive development.

These assessment forms are not meant to serve as a screening instrument or as the basis for a grade placement decision; nor do they replace the report card used in your school. Instead, they help you with the monumental task of compiling and organizing the data you need to teach your students effectively, to provide accurate information to colleagues and parents, and to prepare the many documents and reports required of kindergarten teachers.

At one time, assessment techniques used in the upper grades filtered down into early childhood classrooms. Formal test scores rated against standards for the grade determined the "marks" a child received. This never gave us accurate or useful information about young children, for whom pencil-and-paper tasks in workbooks and on standardized tests are usually uncomfortable and, in some cases, simply impossible.

Fortunately, the tide has turned once again, even in some of the upper grades, and most educators now recognize that basing the assessment of children on standardized test scores is not developmentally appropriate. The "buzz words" today — portfolios, authentic assessment, performance assessment, math and reading inventories — focus on what children are actually achieving in the classroom, rather than how well they complete a series of artificial tasks in a contrived format during a limited period of time. Now, early childhood professionals are at the forefront of the "new wave" in assessment, and we must document our findings in an organized way in order to provide authenticity and accountability.

> *...we must document our findings in an organized way...*

There is a growing consensus as to the purpose and characteristics of this new type of assessment. Most early childhood educators agree that an appropriate assessment should:

> provide baseline information,
> identify individual learning needs,
> document progress over time,
> assess higher-order thinking, communication skills, and problem-solving,
> facilitate instruction and help to evaluate programs.

In addition, an appropriate assessment should have the following characteristics:

it has a continuous, long-term time frame,

it does not disrupt instruction or learning,

it is organized around students and their activities,

it includes the academic, social/emotional, and physical realms.

As I developed my assessment materials and techniques, which grew directly out of my own needs as a kindergarten teacher, I was not aware of formal guidelines such as these. So, I was very pleased when they were recently described to me and I found that my approach matched these guidelines. I believe this sort of experience validates both the guidelines and the approach described on the following pages.

> *...I found that my approach matched these guidelines.*

What's in this for you?

With the elimination of extra-year options in many schools, as well as the increased "inclusion" of children who have special needs, many kindergarten teachers are being told that their job is to "take the children where they are and move them along." This seemingly simple approach, however, requires us to accurately determine "where" the children are and how we can effectively "move" them (in the right direction). Even when extra-year options are available and new students have gone through a rigorous selection process, we still face challenges finding out where our students are starting from and how we can help them progress.

That's why you'll find a *Baseline Assessment Form* used to record information about a child's development and readiness when you and the child are first getting to know each other. It shows strengths and weakness at a glance, and there's a *Year-End Assessment Summary* sheet which reveals much about the progress that has occurred during the year, as well as any "problem areas" which remain.

For use between the beginning and end of the school year, I created a variety of forms and checklists that capture information about important student activities and areas of development. For example, the *Social Characteristics Checklist* helps you gather information when you observe children in a social setting, in order to gain valuable insights about a child's personality. Repeating this a month later will reveal changes that help you assess social growth and make decisions about grouping or "buddying" certain children. In particular, pairing a shy child with a more outgoing child can help promote social skills and enable the shy one to integrate more effectively with the rest of the class.

I also developed simple forms that show the names of students using the different learning centers each day, in order to find out how often children return to one area or flit from one to another. Children tend to choose activities because of a need or interest they have, or because they are following another child's lead. Keeping a record of children's choices, along with information about their social characteristics, shows which children are actively engaged in group play, and which ones prefer to work with materials alone or with only one other child. Is a child in the latter group shy or just a loner by preference? Follow his or her interests and involvements for a few days, and you will find out.

In the cognitive realm, the *Student Development Profile* shows when skills are learned or breakthroughs achieved throughout the year. There are also *Lesson Assessment Forms* which help you track how well children follow the directions and do the work involved in a particular lesson.

Forms such as these enable you to use a "diagnostic-prescriptive" approach. By helping you compile and analyze important information quickly and easily, they enable you make a diagnosis and then draw up a prescription of activities and instruction that will support growth in areas of need.

Other checklists provide similar support by helping you compile information about children's activities at key points during the year. And, there are also materials and information that help you assess children's emerging language skills, such as letter recognition, level of writing, and sight vocabulary.

When used together over the course of the year, the forms, checklists, and information help you with a variety of tasks. You will have a clear profile of each child — including his or her interests, abilities, and needs — which you can share with parents, other educators, and administrators. You will be able to plan your lessons more quickly, complete special-needs assessments more easily, and pair children as buddies or in cooperative-learning groups more effectively. You will have organized vital observational data in an efficient, easy-to-understand format, and, perhaps best of all, you will have accomplished this important task right in your own classroom while your students are with you.

> *You will have a clear profile of each child...*

How can I do all this with the kids in *my* class?

This may sound like a difficult task, but a little planning is all that's required to make written assessment an integral part of your daily routine. Gathering information about the children in your class is something you already are doing every day. The forms and techniques described in this book simply help you do it in an easier and more organized way.

I have found that what works best for me is to walk around with a clipboard on which I have the particular assessment sheet that I plan to concentrate on, as well as a few blank sheets of paper on which I can jot down any unexpected incidents or insights. I may watch the children who play in the Family Center one day and pay attention to the way each child socializes. Or, if I'm working on a *Social Characteristics Checklist*, I may focus on one or two children periodically throughout the day and observe them participating in a variety of activities.

The beginning of the year, when the children are acclimating to school and forming friendships, is obviously the time to collect a wealth of baseline data. Center time provides a good opportunity to observe, as does the Sharing Circle. In both situations, you can see which children can wait their turns and sit still, who seems to be popular or left out, and so on.

Gradually, the focus changes from physical, social, and emotional checks to the cognitive areas, although all areas are reviewed periodically. As we continue to add content to the day, we may need to use specific one-on-one tasks to obtain more detailed assessments of cognitive areas. Such tasks should be simple, short, and non-threatening, showing what children have brought with them and where we should begin to help them grow in developmentally appropriate ways. Information from this sort of task-oriented assessment can then be combined with what we observe as our children interact with materials and other children.

Kindergarten teachers naturally tend to notice all this, but until you put it on paper and add to it each month, you are likely to lose track of the changes that take place over time. Written assessments also help you prompt changes that require your intervention in order to take place — changes that might otherwise become lost opportunities because they won't happen on their own.

By becoming selective and focusing on particular activities and children on given days, you will soon become comfortable with this process, rather than feeling over-burdened by it. And, as the months go by, it will become second nature. There is tremendous flexibility in this approach, which allows you to take advantage of sudden, unexpected opportunities. Just as there is the "teachable moment," there is also the "assessment moment" when an important new observation or insight occurs, and you can simply jot it down on the piece of

...it will become second nature.

blank paper on your clipboard, then transfer it to the appropriate form when you have a quiet minute or two later in the day.

At the end of the year, when we report to parents and to next year's teacher about the progress each child has made, we must be able to look back to the start of the year in order to see where each began and how much growth has occurred. If you have used the sheets and techniques described here, you will be amazed at how clearly each child's development becomes visible to you. The baseline data, combined with other records kept throughout the year, provide a complete profile of this important transitional period in each child's life.

You will also be pleased at how easily the sheets enable you to share information at a parent conference. All of the positive developmental gains will be easy to point out, as will the areas of concern. But, even in the areas of concern, you will have evidence of growth *from where the child started.* (There is always growth, but some children come to us with such huge needs that the growth is slow and needs continual reinforcement.)

And, a summary of the growth plus any areas of concern is easy to pass on to next year's teacher, who can use it as the baseline for the new educational adventure that begins after summer vacation.

> *...you will have evidence of growth...*

Who to watch when (and how and why)?

Kindergarten teachers are always observing behavior patterns and the choices children make, forming a nucleus of understanding of each little person in our charge. It is our responsibility to assess every single child accurately, and we must be vigilant in discovering the child who may be gifted, or the one who needs special help. By now, we are all aware of the importance and effectiveness of early intervention, so an important part of our job is to compile initial information about children who need special assistance either from us or from other specialists.

I make sure to pay particular attention to quiet children who do not make trouble and tend to be ignored because they demand nothing. First of all, we need to determine whether they are quiet because of shyness or just a preference to work alone. Some people are naturally self-sufficient and prefer to work by themselves — whether at age 5 or 55. Children like this need to be noticed with a smile and some quiet conversation, so they are aware that they are important and cared for, and that they can make valuable contributions to the group in their own way.

In contrast, the quiet child who is basically shy needs help in joining the social mainstream of the class. Sometimes, it helps to pair this child with a self-sufficient, friendly child who will help ease the shy child into a group. Recognition of the child's work and worth by the teacher and other students also helps.

Charting the behavior of an anti-social or belligerent child will help in devising a plan for behavior modification. Noting the choices such a child makes and the behaviors that accompany those choices may indicate a pattern. Certain activities might work well for the child, while others need to be off-limits or gradually allowed when accompanied by acceptable behavior.

A similar approach can help the children who are drawn to other children but whose social skills need improvement. Growth and understanding can occur once strengths and weaknesses are noted, and an appropriate plan which supports social development is implemented.

Thoughts and impressions form every time we watch children interact with each other, but essentially they remain unanswered questions until we document what we have observed, analyze the data, and decide on a course of action.

Is this child a consistent leader, or only in certain types of activities?

How does the quiet child with excellent creative arts skills and ideas respond to those who seek to copy his or her creations?

Is the child equally comfortable and capable during language and math activities?

Let's find out, and then do what we can to foster the children's development, knowing that secure, well-adjusted children who enjoy the learning process are far more likely to thrive and succeed as students.

On we go

The pages that follow provide overviews of the assessment areas, followed by photocopy masters of the assessment forms, along with detailed information about their use. How you use the forms is your decision, which should be based on your personal preferences and the type of curriculum in your school. You may want to use the existing materials in the exact same way I do, or make some minor or not-so-minor modifications to fit your needs and teaching style. You may also find that what I have done inspires you to create your own forms and

How you use the forms is your decision...

accompanying techniques, and I would be happy to have contributed to that sort of professional development.

Whatever approach you choose, you will find yourself enjoying the fruits of your labor as you read through your assessments at the end of the school year. There should be great satisfaction in knowing you have been thoroughly professional in carrying out your responsibilities to your children — assessing their needs, responding appropriately, and helping them grow. There is also great personal satisfaction in recognizing how well you have come to know the children, and how much growth has occurred during the kindergarten year.

> *...recognizing how well you have come to know the children...*

Organizing & Using Your Assessment Forms & Checklists

There are a number of ways you can organize your copies of the forms and checklists which appear on the following pages. What works best for you will depend to a large extent on your personal preferences and experience. Here are four possibilities to consider:

A. Put hole-punched copies of the forms and checklists in a looseleaf binder, with tabs identifying each section. Keep these sheets in the order in which they appear in the book, as this provides the easiest access to the directions in the book. You can also color code the sheets and corresponding pages of the book.

B. Keep each set of sheets in a file folder in your desk or file cabinet, either in order or color-coded as described above. It's easier to add pages this way, but not as easy to take all the information with you or have it readily available.

C. Organize the sheets by assessment areas — social, emotional, cognitive, physical. There will be some overlap among the areas and sheets, but this may appeal to teachers who are "global learners."

D. If you have your own individualized approach to record keeping, integrate the sheets into the system that is most familiar and comfortable for you.

The two pages that follow provide an overview of the assessment sheets in this book. The first page lists the sheets and accompanying information in the order in which they appear in the book, while the second page lists the sheets according to the times of year in which they will be used.

Assessment Form Overview

Assessment	Schedule	Usage
Baseline Assessment Form	Prior spring or start of year	Work with children individually for 10-15 minutes
Beginning Activities Checklist	September & October	Observe 2 or 3 children each day during Center Time
Center Participation Form	September, December & March	Group observation, 5 minutes per center
Student Development Profile	September - June	Fill in monthly for each child where applicable
Social Characteristics Checklist	October - November & April - May	General observation of social patterns and interactions
Class Social & Emotional Profile	November & April	Daily observation of a few children & previous observation
Lesson Assessment Form	September - June	Assess individual performance based on class lesson
Word Recognition Form	January - May	Weekly or twice a month during Daily Story or Writer's Table
Mid-Year Activities Checklist	January - February	Observe 2 or 3 children each day during Center Time
Spring Assessment Form	March - April	Work with children individually for 10-15 minutes
Year-End Assessment Summary	May - June	Record data for each child based on observations & assessments
Year-End Special Needs Form	May - June	Data from other forms and general observation

Assessment Calendar

Season	Months	Assessment	Page
Spring	May	*Baseline Assessment Form*	17
Fall	Sept-Oct	*Baseline Assessment Form*	17
	Sept-Oct	*Beginning Activities Checklist*	40
	Sept	*Center Participation Form*	43
	Sept, Oct, Nov	*Lesson Assessment Form*	63
	Sept, Oct, Nov	*Student Development Profile*	48
	Oct-Nov	*Social Characteristics Checklist*	54
	Nov	*Class Social & Emotional Profile*	59
Winter	Dec	*Center Participation Form*	43
	Dec, Jan, Feb	*Lesson Assessment Form*	63
	Dec, Jan, Feb	*Student Development Profile*	48
	Jan, Feb	*Word Recognition Form*	71
	Jan-Feb	*Mid-Year Activities Checklist*	83
Spring	Mar	*Center Participation Form*	43
	Mar, Apr, May, June	*Lesson Assessment Form*	63
	Mar, Apr, May	*Word Recognition Form*	71
	Mar, Apr	*Spring Assessment Form*	87
	Mar, Apr, May, June	*Student Development Profile*	48
	Apr-May	*Social Characteristics Checklist*	54
	Apr	*Class Social & Emotional Profile*	59
	May-June	*Year-End Assessment Summary*	96
	May-June	*Year-End Special Needs Form*	99

Baseline Assessment

If you are fortunate — as I am — to meet your children before school begins, you have a head start on developing a profile of each child. Almost all my children visit during the spring (three at a time) and spend about one-and-a-half hours in class with the kindergarten children.

If your school does not have a spring visitation, you can do a baseline assessment of each child during the first month or two of school. I did it this way for many years. By working with one or two children a day during Center or Play time, you will be able to do the one-on-one tasks I describe below and observe those specific children's social interactions.

Whether in the fall or the previous spring, the information I gather falls into two general categories. One category covers my observations of the child's interactions with other people and materials, including how well the child separates, whether the child appears shy or outgoing, how physically coordinated the child is, how well the child attends, whether the child chooses activities independently, and so on. This information, which might be called the "external component," helps me understand how the child is likely to respond to the kindergarten environment and to act as a member of the class.

In addition to observing the children in this context, I work with each one alone for about ten or fifteen minutes, collecting other data in regard to language development, fine-motor coordination, awareness, and behavior. This information, which might be called the "internal component," helps me obtain a better understanding of the child as an individual learner.

The combination of both types of information — external and internal — gives me a valuable and accurate overview of each child's strengths and weaknesses in key areas of the intellectual, physical, social, and emotional domains. And, this information then enables me to plan more effectively for the class as a whole, as well as to better meet individual children's needs. It also documents the starting point for each child, making it easy to look back later in the year and see how each child has progressed.

When my incoming students are scheduled to visit us in the spring before they start kindergarten, they join the class during Sharing and Center time. This provides opportunities to observe each visitor in the social setting that Center interaction offers, and it lets me spend time alone with each visitor while the others are involved with an activity such as painting, blocks, drawing, puzzles, etc. The only drawback I've found with this approach is holding the attention of the child I am working with while the rest of the class is playing, but that, too, is a clue to the child's ability to separate from one activity and focus on another.

I let the three visitors choose which area they want to play in, and I start working individually with whichever child is last to make a choice. However, some visiting children need to be near me the entire time, in which case I make room for them nearby and give them crayons and paper or some puzzles to do, while I work individually with the others. I encourage social play and painting, but not all little ones can handle that during their first visit to a classroom filled with older children.

Each visitor spends about ten minutes just with me, and usually this is an enjoyable time. The children like having the individual attention of the teacher focused on their interests and family. And, it's nice for me to able to focus on one child and start building a rapport, even for just a few minutes.

Of course, my eyes are all over the room during this time, especially if I'm the only adult. I do explain to my class beforehand what I expect from them when the visitors come, and what they should do with the visitors. (They are to be kind and helpful, show the visitors where things are, etc.) I also explain that I should not be interrupted, except in an emergency, and I remind the class that they came to visit a year ago, when I spent the same time with them that I am now going to spend with our new visitors.

Guidelines for the *Baseline Assessment Form*

...it can be completed quickly in the classroom...

This form helps you compile the results of the screening done with each child before school begins or at the start of the school year. It organizes the information so that it is easy to review and gives you a profile of each child individually, as well as in comparison with classmates. And, using the brief procedures and simple coding system described below, along with the *Baseline Assessment Worksheet* which appears on page 25, it can be completed quickly in the classroom during the school day.

Children's names and birthdates can be filled in ahead of time, based on the class list and any records or parent questionnaires the school has compiled. (I list the children's names in alphabetical order, so they're easy to find.) These sources should also enable you to note whether or not the child has attended preschool

Baseline Assessment Form

Name	Birthdate	Attends preschool	Can draw shapes	Can write name	Can write numbers	Can draw a figure	Knows birthday	Speech/language	Knows colors	Fine-motor coordination	Socialization	Gross-motor coord.	Perception	Comments

or your school's summer program, if one exists. This information simply helps me put the rest of the data in a proper perspective.

I obtain the rest of the data through conversation, observation, and the responses to a series of simple, non-threatening tasks that I present individually to each visitor. Some are derived from the Gesell Developmental Assessments and show me the level of development at which a child is currently functioning. Other tasks provide additional information, helping me develop an overall assessment of where a child is in each given area at this point in time, based on strengths and weaknesses easily identifiable in the child's own work.

The child and I sit at a table where I have all of my materials ready, including the *Baseline Assessment Worksheet* where I make my initial notes during the session. I give the child a blank sheet of paper and a pencil. Then, I ask the child to draw what I show, as I present a series of 5" x 7" cards, each of which has one of the following shapes:

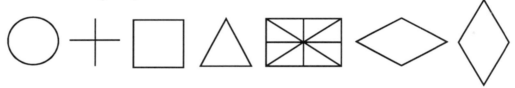

Children who are five-years-old can usually draw a recognizable circle, square, and triangle, although some have difficulty with the triangle's points. Children of this age can also draw a rectangle, which may look like a square, but usually the intersecting lines are replaced by three horizontal lines on each side of a center vertical line, as shown below:

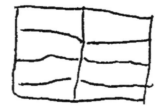

Diamonds are very difficult for five-year-olds, but most children do attempt to draw them.

Children who draw intersecting lines within the rectangle and somewhat recognizable diamonds are demonstrating behavior beyond that of a typical five-year-old. Children who have difficulty with the triangle and rectangle (and sometimes the square) — making all shapes circular and without corners — are exhibiting skills that have not yet reached a five-year-old level.

As I first see the children in the spring, and our cut-off date for kindergarten entrance in New York State is December 1st, many of the children are four-and-a-half or four-and-three-quarters at this time. Obviously, whatever your state's cut-off date for kindergarten entrance, it's important to consider the child's birthday and whether the drawings are age-appropriate, immature, or mature for children of that specific age.

I also take note of the pencil grip and pencil control, considering the following questions:

> *Is the child comfortable using a pencil?*
> *Is the grip natural or unusual?*
> *Is it a three, four, or five-fingered (fist-like) grasp?*
> *Are the strokes firm or wavery?*
> *What is the quality of the work of this young child?*

You can usually get a sense of whether the child uses pencils and paper at home, or if these materials seem new and alien. When a child has not had experience with the materials, just using them becomes the child's primary focus, rather than drawing the shapes. Some children find pencils difficult to handle at this age, but have no problem with crayons.

All of this must be observed and noted, because the drawings are influenced by a variety of factors which must be taken into account. To expand on the example just cited, a weak, wavering stroke might at first appear to indicate weak fine-motor coordination, when it may result from a lack of familiarity with the writing instrument being used.

Another clue to the level of development is where these shapes are placed on the blank sheet of paper. The Gesell Institute's research has shown that five-year-olds tend to make a large circle in the center of the paper and draw the other shapes around the circle, in a smaller size. Five-and-a-half-year-olds begin to line the shapes up, and may put the first three in a row, with the circle in the middle and another shape on either side. Children younger than five may need more than one sheet of paper, sometimes one for each shape. (For more information, see the book, *School Readiness,* listed on the Resource page.)

After completing the shapes, I ask the children to write their name if they can. Most incoming kindergarten students who have attended preschool can write their name. Others who can't write their name may never have been shown how. When children say they cannot, I ask them what the first letter in their name is, and if they know, I ask if they can write just that letter.

If a child is unable to write any letters, I write the name on another sheet of paper and ask the child to copy it. This shows me if the children can form letters, if they are perceiving them as they were written, and if they recognize those particular letters, so I have a sense of whether there may be a motor or perception problem.

Lastly, I ask each child if he or she knows any numbers and can write them on the same sheet of paper. When children say they cannot, I specifically ask if they can write a 1, a 2, and a 3. If children say they cannot write a 2 or 3, I then ask if they can write a 7 or 8, as these numbers seem to be known by many children who can only write very few numbers.

Kindergarten-age children demonstrate a wide range of abilities in this area, from being able to write numbers 1 through 20 with no reversals, to having no comprehension of what a numeral looks like. The numerals 2 and 3 are the hardest for young children to reproduce and are usually reversed, while 6 and 9 are often confused for each other.

The average five-year-old can write numbers 1 through 5, or at least a recognizable 1, 7, 8 if prompted. A child who writes numbers 1 through 10 is showing a developmental level of five-and-a-half. No number awareness in the written form indicates a developmental level below five-years-old in this domain, although some children have simply never been shown how to write numbers and quickly learn to do so when taught.

These are the tasks I ask each child to do on the first unlined sheet of paper. The entire process actually takes five minutes at most, depending on how willing the child is, how comfortable the child is with a pencil, and how well the child can sit still and focus on the task at hand. Meanwhile, I am also observing the child's attention span, ability to follow directions, and ability to tune out other activities taking place in the classroom.

Next, I give the child another blank sheet of paper and ask him or her to draw a person. If a child needs help just completing a head, I sometimes provide clues such as, "Where are his eyes?" or "Does he have hair?" The results will range from just a head with or without facial features and hair, to a head with arms and legs radiating out of it, to a head with some form of body beneath it — from a stick figure to a fully shaped body.

Obviously, the extent of the resemblance and details provide indications of maturation. I use a ✓ to note a child who draws a recognizable stick figure or

> *The entire process actually takes five minutes...*

full figure, a question mark to note a child who draws feet and arms radiating from a round head, and an **X** to note a child who can only draw a head or less than that.

This exercise also provides information about a child's awareness of body parts, as well as his or her pencil control. As you work with more and more of your children, a quick glance will give you an idea of the child's current level of development, and a quick review of all the drawings you collect gives you a sense of the full range of developmental levels you will have in your classroom.

The next series of tasks help me assess each child's language and knowledge. I ask the child, "When is your birthday?" and if the child does not know, I ask what month it is in, or whether it is in winter or summer.

What we are looking for here is whether the child has any understanding of dates, months, or times of year. One child answered, "Christmas," and sure enough it was December 25th, but the child did not know the date.

A child who answers with complete accuracy receives a ✓ in the appropriate column on the *Baseline Assessment Form*, while someone who just knows the right month will have "mo" in his or her column. I use an **X** to note anyone who seems to have no accurate knowledge.

Then I ask the child what he or she likes to do best at school and at home, and I record these responses. Children are so ego-centric at this age, they usually enjoy these questions and answers about their own interests and family. And, according to research compiled by the Gesell Institute, children's responses to these questions are a good indicator of their current stage of development.

> *...they usually enjoy these questions and answers...*

For example, in answer to the question, "What do you like to do best?", the typical five-year-old will say, "Play!", the typical six-year-old might say, "Work!", and a five-and-one-half-year-old will say, "Play!" and then add what he or she likes to play with. In addition to providing clues about each child's developmental level, these questions along with follow-up inquiries can provide valuable information about the child's interests and activities.

During this conversation, I am also listening to the child's speech patterns, vocabulary, communication skills, responsiveness to the specific question asked, ability to sustain, body language (sits, squirms, bobs up and down, stands), ability to focus, and general demeanor. Again, Gesell research indicates typical behaviors for each age, but any experienced teacher will be able to use these personal observations to help determine if the child seems advanced, in need of help, and ready overall for the kindergarten year. In addition, familiarity with these characteristics of each child is extremely helpful in planning large and small group activities for the year.

Most of all, this conversation provides me with a basis for assessing the child's speech and language. I put a ✓ on the *Baseline Assessment Form* if the speech and language are fine, and a question mark if I am unsure, noting any distortions or problems in the Comments column. If the child is very hard to understand or seems deficient in language, I put an **X** in the Speech/Language column, with an accompanying explanation. This would include any children who consistently did not understand my questions or could not follow directions, as well as those who do not speak English well, or have limited speech but seem to understand what I say.

Any child who has a **?** or an **X** in the Speech/Language column should be referred to a Speech/Language therapist for further evaluation.

The last part of this screening involves a sheet of paper with a big circle drawn on it and eight differently colored crayons. I ask the child what each color is as I point to a crayon, and if the child has difficulty answering, I say something like, "Can you show me the red crayon?" to see if the child can find it when it is labeled.

I put a ✓ in the Knows Colors column if a child knows all or most colors, and an **X** if the child knows few colors or none. A child who receives an **X** — and who still doesn't know the colors after you've introduced and worked with them — may need to be tested by the nurse for color-blindness. If that's not the problem, enlist the help of the parents in organizing "red days" or "blue days" at home, so that the child has help identifying all the things in the house that are one particular color. The same thing can also be done at school.

> *...enlist the help of the parents...*

I then tell the child to color in the circle. Some children handle a crayon much more comfortably than they handle a pencil. Most five-year-olds color in the entire circle, using one or some or all of the colors. (Girls, especially, tend to make an art project out of this task.) Very young children scribble lines in the circle, ignore the circle shape, or draw just one round line inside the circle. Sometimes, a face will be drawn, which indicates that the child may have trouble understanding or following directions.

The work with the crayon, combined with the earlier writing and drawing work, provides the basis for the entry in the Fine-Motor Coordination column.

I put in a ✓ if the child's ability is age-appropriate, an **X** if the ability is poor, and a **?** if I am unsure — as when there are wavery lines with a pencil but the control is okay with a crayon. A child in the latter two categories will need many opportunities to work with scissors, paste, and paint under your supervision when school begins.

I thank the child for working with me and ask what he or she would like to play with now. My kindergarten students are involved in Learning Center activities at this time, so there is a wide range of options available. If the child does not answer, I suggest activities such as painting or drawing with markers, which are usually accepted and can be done right near where I am sitting. Other children can't wait to get to the Blocks or Family centers, having grown antsy working with me.

I try to pay careful attention to behavior in the centers, as this provides important information about the child. You are watching the child to see how he or she integrates and relates to others. However, there can be a big difference between doing this in the spring, when the child is just visiting the class, and doing it in the fall, when the child is a member of the class. A springtime visitor may be too shy to socialize with older strangers, but do fine in the fall amongst classmates.

In the socialization column, I use a ✓ if the child does well, a **?** if I'm unsure about the social skills, and an **X** if the child needs help. With either a **?** or an **X**, there should be a brief note in the Comments column.

In the meantime, while the children are interacting or engaged in activities, I observe gross-motor coordination (just an overall impression based on the child's movement around the room and any relevant activities), social interaction, choice of activities, and task completion (does the child's attention span allow an activity to be worked on and completed, or does the child flit from one area to another?).

Once the child becomes involved in another activity, I finish compiling the key assessment information on my worksheet. This includes whether the child could draw the shapes — particularly the divided rectangle; could write his name and numbers; and knew his birthday, and his colors. Other key data includes my observations of his fine-motor coordination, speech and language patterns, attention span, ability to attend, and perception.

> *I thank the child for working with me...*

Your evaluation of the last category should be based on your overall observations. Again, I use a ✓ if a child's perception seems fine, a **?** if I'm not sure, and an **X** if there's a definite problem. A **?** might be necessary if you could not effectively screen the child, due to a language problem, a refusal to cooperate, or shyness. Either an **X** or a **?** should generate a note in the Comments column.

While this may sound difficult and tedious, it actually can be done quickly and easily if you jot the information down in an abbreviated form. Here's a sample of my notation system with some examples, as well as additional explanations for you in parentheses:

> bd (birthday) - ✓, mo (month), **X**
> socialization - ✓, **?**, **X**
> fine-motor - ✓, **?**, **X**
> sp (speech) - "L" (has trouble pronouncing "L")
> lang (language) - ✓, **?**, **X**
> colors - ✓, **?**, **X**
> figure - ✓, **?**, **X**
> shapes - ✓, **?**, **X**
> name - ✓, **?**, **X**
> #s - ✓, **?**, **X**   1-5
> gross-motor - ✓, **?**, **X**
> perception - ✓, **?**, **X**

In addition, I often have some other notes like the following, which I may or may not include in the Comments column:

> att span (attention span) short in structured setting
> attends for 1st 5 minutes

When I have time during the day, I transfer this information from my worksheet to my *Baseline Assessment Form.*

Following are some additional questions I consider during this time:

> *Does the child engage in conversation, play with others, or work alone?*
>
> *If the child paints, what does the quality of the painting reveal about the child's maturity level?*
>
> *If the child works with a puzzle, can the child complete it independently, and if help is needed, will the child ask for help?*
>
> *Does the child seem comfortable in this environment?*

Baseline Assessment Worksheet

Name _____   Date _____   Birthdate _____

	Notation	Comments
birthday		
socialization		
fine-motor		
speech		
language		
colors		
figure		
shapes		
name		
numbers		
gross-motor		
perception		
attention span		
attends		

Did the parent remain because the child couldn't separate, and if so, was the child able to join in with other children, or did the child stay close to Mom the entire time?

All of this information is noted on my worksheet and then used to determine the notations I make on the *Baseline Assessment Form*. Any above-average or at-risk behaviors, along with other pertinent information, is noted in the "Comments" section of the *Baseline Assessment Form*. I keep the worksheets and the students' drawings until later in the year, as they are sometimes helpful to refer to.

The baseline data on the sheet will show at a glance the overall composition of your incoming class, as well as each child's developmental level in specific areas. At my school, after the initial visits and screening by the special services staff are completed, we meet and share our findings. As you might expect, a completed *Baseline Assessment Form* proves very helpful at this meeting.

Any child that you are really concerned about in one or more areas should be designated AT RISK in the Comments column. I use a yellow highlighter to make those two words stand out on the page. If you do not have a scheduled meeting to review findings, you should bring this information to the appropriate personnel — a specialist, the building child-study team, an administrator, special ed. director, etc. Make your concerns known! The sooner you do this, the sooner you can get help for the child.

Sometimes, when we see that a child has a serious problem, we call in the parents and recommend special services for their child, or sometimes even a special class. Our school has a summer program for incoming students, so we also provide information to the summer staff about children to watch, those we need more information about, and those who excelled in a specific area and so will need enriched activities. Children who have speech problems work with the Speech Therapist during the summer and usually continue to do so in the fall.

For your own use as a teacher, the *Baseline Assessment Form* takes apart the "whole picture" in order to provide specific information about important aspects of each child's development. However, once this is done, a comprehensive picture of the whole child emerges, and you are well-prepared to gear pertinent activities to each child's needs as the year unfolds. And, you can compare this data with the information on the *Spring Assessment From* to see what progress has been made.

> *Make your concerns known!*

Open-ended lessons and activities, which allow for the developmental range in your class, will enable each child to be successful in his or her own way. Providing creative materials will enable each child to work at his or her own level, while developing problem-solving techniques and skills. For example, scissors and paste are basic tools children use in countless ways and find much pleasure in using. But, a child who has difficulty handling scissors needs to be taught how and then helped to succeed, in order to derive pleasure from this activity. Then, it is a tremendous thrill for the child to master the skill and for us as teachers to help the child experience the excitement and joy of learning.

> *...it is a tremendous thrill for the child to master the skill...*

As with the other assessment sheets, there may be additional information you want to record on the *Baseline Assessment Form,* as well as information I record that does not seem necessary or relevant to you. Feel free to modify my sheet or create a new one of your own. The key is to find a comfortable way to assess new students, and record your observations in a way that provides accountability and is easily understood by others.

Assessing Students' Initial Activities

You can start assessing your students' initial activities right from the first day of school. As soon as you start getting to know your new students, you instinctively begin noticing different students' capabilities, patterns of behavior, and preferences. Rather than just keeping all this important information in your head, the *Beginning Activities Checklist* helps you organize and record your observations, so that you have permanent and accurate initial data on your children, and you can determine how best to respond to them.

As mentioned in the previous section on Baseline Assessment, I am fortunate in being able to meet incoming students before the start of the school year, so I can prepare my *Baseline Assessment Checklist* at that time. This leaves me (relatively) free to work on the *Beginning Activities Checklist* in September. Teachers who are meeting children for the first time at the start of the school year may find they need to focus just on Baseline Assessment during the first few busy weeks of school. However, alternating between Baseline and Beginning Activities Assessment at different times of the school day makes your initial data more comprehensive and accurate, as well as available to you that much sooner.

Your introduction of kindergarten routines, materials, and activities is a vital part of your students' learning process, and a great opportunity for you to make your initial observations. As the routines, materials, and activities I use in my classroom will be referred to throughout this book, this section includes some information about my introductory process, so that you have a better understanding of my classroom and teaching methods, and you can see how the assessment process for the *Beginning Activities Checklist* is integrated with the first two weeks of school.

In my school, kindergarten lasts only half a day, and the first two sessions are only two hours long. While I teach separate morning and afternoon sessions, I will just use the word "morning" in this section.

Prior to the first day of school, I put each child's name on the "cubby" where his or her things will be stored, put up bulletin board displays, and hang a "Welcome to Kindergarten" sign on the classroom door. I also put an assortment of materials on each table, including drawing paper and crayon boxes, puzzles, pegs and peg boards, books, and beads and string. These materials and the children's reactions to them become the basis for some of the initial data recorded on the *Beginning Activities Checklist.*

When the children arrive for the first day of school, any materials or smocks they bring are put into the marked cubbies, which provides me with an opportunity to find out if they can recognize their written name. I then invite them to sit around the tables wherever they wish, and to begin working with whatever material they like. As children in such a new environment are likely to choose an activity that they know and enjoy, their initial choices provide information about their preferences and past experience.

While the children work, I rotate around the tables, making sure that every child is busy. Whenever anyone finishes a picture, I ask if they can write their name on the back of it, before it goes into the "going home" basket. Their verbal response, as well as their ability do so if they can, can be quite revealing.

Most children entering my class in recent years have been able to write their name, usually in capital letters. However, some children say that they can, but what they write bears little or no resemblance to all the letters in their name. This is an important clue as to what these children perceive themselves as capable of doing. I remember one little boy who proudly said, "Yes, here's my name!" and boldly wrote a large *R* on the back of his picture. That was exactly how he thought Robert was spelled.

When children say they cannot write their name, I ask them if they can "make" the first letter in their name. Often, they can, and then the other letters follow when prompted in the same way. If they truly cannot, I write their name for them, and then I know that with each piece of work they will need to be shown how and helped. The name tag in their crayon boxes can serve as a model to copy from, and children who have difficulty copying letters can be taught one letter at a time, which is easier to learn and less threatening.

As each child finishes a project, I ask what he or she would like to do next, and I then bring that choice to the child. In this way, their preferences and patterns of behavior begin to emerge.

After twenty minutes or so, when the children start getting restless, I tell them to stop and listen for a minute while I take attendance. I say, "Good morning," followed by a child's first name, and I encourage each child to respond in

> *I then invite them to sit around the tables...*

a similar way — "Good morning, Mrs. Keshner." Even this simple activity can provide important information about a child's personality and verbal ability.

I then count the children and perhaps do a couple of finger plays, before telling the children to continue their work at the tables. I continue to rotate around them as described earlier, jotting down a few notes when possible, until another break is needed. At that point, I have all the children stop what they are doing and come to the piano, where they sit in a large circle. I play *Thumbkin* and *Open, Shut Them*, then sing the following song:

> My name is Mrs. Keshner, Keshner, Keshner,
> My name is Mrs. Keshner, and who are you?

I point to the child on my left, who hopefully says his or her name, which I repeat and then use in the song. This process continues as we proceed to each child in the circle, until it's my turn again and I end by singing:

> My name is Mrs. Keshner, Keshner, Keshner,
> My name is Mrs. Keshner, and how do you do?
> Welcome to kindergarten!

Just like taking attendance, this activity provides information about children's personalities and verbal abilities. Some children won't say their name, because school is too new and they feel shy. Others can't wait to have their turn. Fortunately, all my kids wear name tags during the first day, so I can fill in each child's name if I have to, without making a fuss or missing a beat.

This activity also provides me with a nice lead-in to a discussion about kindergarten and what we will be doing. After that, we have another session at the tables, during which I pay particular attention to the drawings.

Children who make recognizable shapes tend to be more advanced, while those who make scribbles or cover the entire paper with color tend to be younger chronologically and/or developmentally. It takes some degree of maturity for a child to see the possibilities of pictures other than solid masses of color. However, sometimes children will draw a delightful picture (by adult standards) and then continue to color until every bit of the paper is covered. Only then are they satisfied, and I chuckle to myself at how unconcerned they are at the loss of the original work of art.

Drawings and paintings become more sophisticated and detailed as the children mature and have daily access to art activities and materials, along with

> *I chuckle to myself at how unconcerned they are...*

freedom to explore and no pressure to produce a specific image. It's the creative process that makes this activity a valuable learning experience, and this process needs to be experienced again and again.

I collect everything as it's completed, and we then prepare to have our first snack together. This is followed by a rest period, stretching exercises, a discussion of playground rules, and some playground time if the weather is good. We return to the classroom in time for me to tell the "The Three Bears" story by the piano, and discuss plans for the following day. Finally, I give everyone back the pictures they made, line them up, and dismiss them for the day, telling them what to expect when they arrive tomorrow and that new things will be happening each day in school.

On the second day, the children come in and sit anywhere, but now nothing is on the tables. After attendance and an initial attempt to recite the Pledge of Allegiance, we sing "America" and our "Greeting Song:"

> Good Morning to you, good morning to you,
> We're all in our places with sunshiny faces,
> Oh, this is the way to start a good day.

After that, I explain how to take puzzles from the rack and put them back, and I also show the children where other manipulatives "live" on the shelf.

The children are also shown where the crayons and drawing paper are kept, and when time permits, we work on writing children's names on their personal crayon boxes, which can then "live" in their personal cubbies. Boxes without names are returned to their storage area. As on the previous day, I encourage the children to either write their names on the back of completed drawings or ask me to help them do so.

When it's time for a change, I introduce the children to the Block Center and explain the rules carefully — blocks taken out must be returned when building is finished, with all the blocks that look the same staying together (the beginning of classification). Depending on the time available and the level of activity, I may also introduce the Family Center and allow children to move freely from one center to another, as long as they clean up their own messes. (See the next section of this book for more information about learning centers and related assessment.)

This free choice time continues until I see the children starting to grow restless. Then, I play a signal on the piano — or turn off the lights — and explain

...new things will be happening each day in school.

that this means it's time to clean up. Depending on the situation, we either discuss what goes where, or I actually help put things back.

As you have probably noticed, an important theme for the second day is the emphasis on cleaning up and putting things back in their proper place. This is not just a vital aspect of classroom management, it is also an important indicator of individual students' impulsivity, distractibility, or responsibility, as well as their ability and willingness to follow directions.

The rest of the second day consists of snack, rest, stretching, a review of the playground rules, and then some time at the playground, followed by a return to the classroom for a story. After that, it's time to pack up and go home.

On the third day of school, we start our Sharing Circle, if most children can "attend" well. (Already, the schedule of activities is being influenced by my assessment of the children.) The children sit in a circle on the floor near the piano, where each child has a turn to show and/or tell, while everyone else listens and demonstrates their good manners. Whenever anyone talks out of turn, I explain how they should behave. And, I make sure to praise the good listeners.

> *...I make sure to praise the good listeners.*

The third day of school is also when I introduce our three-sided easel, which is great for large classes because it allows three children to paint at the same time. I've already prepared three cans of red paint before the children arrive, and on this day we work only with the color red. I paint a large red circle without wiping the brush and talk about what can happen with paint, especially drips and messes. Then, I wipe the brush one, two, three times inside the can and paint another circle, coloring it in fully.

We talk about a circle and describe it, and we also talk about the color red and which things might be red. I then ask the children what my painting could be and write their words on the painting or a separate piece of paper, under the heading, "Many Varied And Unusual Words To Describe This Painting." I also tell the children that everyone will have a turn to paint with the color red today or the following day.

Like their drawings, the children's paintings provide opportunities for assessment, as the older ones make recognizable shapes, while the younger ones tend to cover the entire paper with paint. Among the older children, some copy exactly what I modeled, while others know just what they want to do and exhibit considerable concentration during the process. A few children ask me to write a dictated story, phrase, or word on their painting. Younger children often spend a long time at the easel, filling the paper with paint and getting great satisfaction out of the tactile experience. On occasion, hands get into the act along with paintbrushes.

For the rest of the day, we continue to establish our routines, and I take advantage of opportunities to review the rules for the toy shelf, Block Center, Family Center, and so on. After play time, clean-up, snack, rest, and outdoor play, we read the *Three Bears* big book and try acting it out just before it's time to go home.

On the fourth day, I introduce the calendar after attendance, and we talk about months, days, dates, and holidays. This leads into a discussion of the Helper Chart (shown below — I make mine out of 18" x 24" oak tag), which I've already prepared and put up. I then introduce our helpers for the week, and we talk about each job and what responsibility that job's helper has.

Helper Chart

Messengers	John	Jill
Flag		
Napkins		
Easel		
Family Center		
Library		
Blocks		
Toy Shelf		

You'll see that there are two blanks for messengers, because there are always two children who do this job together, so that a child never leaves the room alone. The flag helper holds the flag during the Pledge of Allegiance, and the napkins helper gives out napkins when snack time begins. The helpers responsible for the Family Center, blocks, library, and toy shelf all make sure during clean-up time that everything is put away neatly.

Every Monday, I change the chart and put the names of new helpers next to each job. (I have each child's name written on a separate piece of red construction paper, which stays in my desk when not on the chart.) I keep a record of which child is given which job, so by June every child has had at least one turn with each job. You can use the accompanying *Weekly Helpers Checklist* to compile this information.

After we finish talking about the Helper Chart, we take a class walk to the office to see where the attendance sheet goes, and where the secretary and principal work. We also visit the nurse, the gym, and the computer room.

When we return to our room, we have Sharing if the children aren't too restless, or we just begin play time. New things are always introduced just before play time, so the children can have immediate access to them, and on this day I introduce the classroom library and the chalkboard, reviewing rules for both areas. I also remind the children who haven't yet painted that it's their turn today. As I take finished paintings off the easel, I try to do a quick assessment of each one, and make sure the artist's name is in the top left corner on the front of the painting. (You can't turn a wet painting over in order to write a name on the back.)

Again, the rest of the routine is clean-up, snack, rest, outside play, story, and dismissal.

By the fifth day, the regular routine has been established, and the days begin to flow along more smoothly, providing more time for assessment. The only change worth noting on the fifth day is that I introduce the color blue at the easel and draw two circles — one blue and one red — before discussing what they could be and how to wipe drips. After the discussion, I add a squiggly tail to each circle, showing how easily the circle can be turned into a balloon.

On the sixth day, I introduce paste along with torn pieces of red and blue scrap paper. The white paste is in plastic containers, and I teach the children how to use ice cream sticks and spread the paste like butter — smoothly and with no lumps. This activity provides a good opportunity to assess the child's concentration and fine-motor skills, which are needed to create artwork that does not ooze paste.

> *Expect messes, and you won't be disappointed!*

This is some children's first experience with pasting, and they can't get enough of it. Expect messes, and you won't be disappointed! The very young children are more interested in feeling the paste all over their fingers than the

Weekly Helpers Checklist

Name	Messengers	Flag	Napkins	Easel	Family Center	Library	Blocks	Toy Shelf		

process of pasting one object onto another. That comes later, so be patient and keep modeling. (Kindergarten teachers are usually very patient with "yucky" stuff, because we recognize the importance of these sensory experiences for our little ones.) It takes a certain amount of dexterity, coordination, and understanding to be able to paste neatly, but by winter all children should reach this goal.

The seventh day is when I introduce green paint at the easel and add green paper to the supplies used for pasting. I also introduce the clay and clay boards, and explain the rules governing their use.

On the eighth day, I introduce blunt-edged scissors, showing the children how to hold them, how to cut, and how to pass them safely to other children. We draw green circles, cut them out, tape them to ice cream sticks, and play with our make-believe lollipops. Paper cutting provides yet another good assessment opportunity, enabling you to differentiate between who can handle scissors, and those who need help.

Some children may have difficulty working with scissors because their parents were afraid to let them have any. A mature child who has not previously used scissors will take to cutting with ease once shown how. A developmentally young child may not be able to grasp the scissors and cut, even with one-on-one help. Further development of coordination is needed, and this will occur in time. Meanwhile, just helping the child with the grip and showing how to hold the paper in relation to the scissors is important, as is demonstrating how to get around corners by cutting in from two sides rather than trying to turn the scissors in the middle of the paper.

This, too, is a learning process, and the end result is secondary to the process itself.

> *...the end result is secondary to the process itself.*

Another activity we start on the eighth day is our first class book — *What I Like Best About School*. Each child picks their favorite thing and draws a picture, and then I write what the child dictates. Next, the pages are fastened together with a cover, and I read the book to the class at the end of the day.

On the ninth day, I introduce yellow at the easel. Now, the more advanced children can paint a picture featuring grass, a blue sky, the sun, and red and yellow flowers.

This is also the day when we start work on the *My Family* books. The children draw pictures of their Moms on 9" x 12" manila paper, and talk about what she does, how she helps, and why they need her. On following days, the children draw other family members (Dad, siblings, themselves, pets, grandparents, etc.) and have similar discussions about different kinds of families and their members. Then, we attach covers which feature the author's name and the date of the book's completion.

These books are of great interest on Meet Your Teacher night. And, when the children make a second version during the spring — in time to be taken home for Mother's Day — the two books become a great way to assess the growth that has occurred during the year. (Hold onto the first set until early May. Together, the books make a much appreciated Mother's Day gift.)

The tenth day is when we begin talking about safety. We draw and paint traffic lights, and discuss rules for going safely to and from school. This discussion continues over several days, and as a related activity we graph and illustrate the different ways children come to school.

Guidelines for the *Beginning Activities Checklist*

During the third week of school, you can be well on your way to completing your *Beginning Activities Checklist*. For the first two weeks, you can be using your checklist or putting check marks next to the names on your class lists — along with a brief comment or two — when the children participate in specific activities such as painting, pasting, and cutting. Then, as the children settle into the routine and a little more time becomes available, you can start transferring this information to the checklist if you haven't been using the checklist all along.

To fill out the checklist, simply list your children's names in the column on the left side, and add any unlisted activities from your classroom on top of the columns to the right. Then, put a check mark in the appropriate columns for each child and write additional information in the Comments column.

Using this information, plus any observation notes or *Center Participation Forms* from the first two weeks of school, you will be able to identify the activities each child is drawn to. Some children may have many areas checked, while others have only a few. What you're looking for are the initial interests of each child, which can then be compared to the interests shown by mid-year and year-end. These are non-judgmental data, which can also include brief comments about abilities or problems.

For example, you may have a child who loves to paste or cut but needs help, so you would put a check in the Cutting/Pasting column and a brief note in the

> *...you will be able to identify the activities each child is drawn to.*

Comments section, which serves as a reminder to work with the child at Playtime in order to find ways to master the task. Then, when you review the checklist later in the year, you will also have valuable information about the child's accomplishments and growth.

The checklist would be filled out in a similar way for a child who frequently needs help in order to finish a puzzle. While some children finish puzzles with ease, other children move pieces around randomly or don't yet seem to understand how to guess which piece goes where. To help a child like this, you can point out the shape of an empty area and ask, "What piece looks like this?" A child who can't grasp this process even with assistance needs a puzzle with fewer pieces, and if that doesn't help, the child may need to be checked for a visual perception problem.

Completing the checklist will also help you identify children who love to use the Library and Listening Centers, but not the more social areas such as the Blocks or Family Centers. You might want to suggest that these children visit the social areas paired with a friend. The experience might open up new vistas for them, or a child may refuse and be perfectly comfortable with his or her choice.

When you share the information from this checklist with parents at a fall conference, you will realize how much you know about the child, and so will the parents. Later in the year, when you compare this checklist with newer data you have compiled, you will see the changes and growth that have occurred, as well as the areas on which you still need to work with each child.

> *...you will realize how much you know about the child...*

Beginning Activities
Checklist

Name	Blocks	Family Center	Cutting, Pasting	Drawing	Painting	Clay	Puzzles	Chalkboard	Library	Listening Center	Manipulatives	Science		Comments

Assessing Learning Center Participation

The Learning Centers in my room at the beginning of the school year are typical of those found in developmentally appropriate kindergartens. While they remain available to the children all year, the material within them changes frequently, often in concert with the theme of the week or the month.

The Family Center may become a doctor's office, a store, a library, or a restaurant, depending on the children's interests and the "stuff" I add to it. The buildings in the Block Area also change as I add trucks, planes, villages, and so on, while the children use their limitless imaginations.

The Science and Math Centers change as new units are introduced and new skills are taught. The Science Center contains some materials that remain for most of the year, such as magnets and magnifying glasses, while other materials like leaves, pumpkins, and seedlings come and go.

The Art Center changes with the addition of markers, watercolor paints, finger paints, different sizes and textures of paper, collage materials, etc. These materials are gradually introduced over time and then left out for the children to make use of as they wish.

The Puppet Theatre and Flannel Board have additional materials added in conjunction with different thematic units. These additions include new shapes and "community helpers" at the Flannel Board, as well as appropriate puppets at the Theatre. And, the children also make and use their own puppets at different times.

The Library Center has new books added to it constantly. So does the Listening Center, which also receives new tapes on a regular basis.

All these Centers encourage the development of language, as well as interaction both with materials and with other children. The Centers help children grow physically, socially, emotionally, and cognitively, while also stimulating creativity, critical thinking, decision making, and problem solving.

To provide these benefits, Center activities need to be open-ended. Centers based on ditto sheets, workbooks, and teacher-directed activities are not appropriate for kindergarten, in my opinion. Interaction with materials and classmates in a child's own way is the goal of Center activities, as is learning by doing, by discovering, by making mistakes, and by taking risks.

I am a firm believer in letting children decide where and how to play during Center time. As long as the children do not disrupt other children's play and follow the rules for Center time (Clean up your own mess before going to another Center, do not mess up other children's work, share and be friendly), they are free to choose their activities in my classroom.

This makes Center time one of the most important parts of the kindergarten day, if not the most important part. At no other time are the children expected to make decisions about where to work and what to do, plan how to use their time, and make a variety of other choices, as well.

The only "assignment" I give all the children during Center time comes at the beginning of the year, when they must paint with each new color added to the easel. As explained in the chapter on Assessing Initial Activities, we work with each new color for two days, and each child has a turn to paint with that color, as well as any previously introduced. Once all the colors have been introduced, the children can decide whether to do easel painting and what colors to use.

> *Children tend to seek an activity that is comfortable...*

Children tend to seek an activity that is comfortable and meets a need. If and when some children have difficulty making choices, I suggest two activities to choose between — an active one such as building with blocks and a quiet one such as painting. Then, we build up to three or more choices over time, as the child becomes more comfortable with decision making.

I may also ask, "What is your plan for today?" and then say, "When you finish, come tell me about your work. Then, clean up and think up another plan for what you want to do next." This is a modification of High Scope's Plan, Do, Review procedure for children's work time. (See High Scope's *Young Children in Action* on the Resource page.)

Guidelines for using the *Center Participation Forms*

These forms provide a quick, simple way to record children's choices during Center time. Concentrating on a few Centers for several days or a week will help you identify the child who consistently chooses one area to play in, as well as the child whose name appears only once or twice in each Center but seems to pop into every Center over time.

Center Participation Form

Center_____ Date_____

Center_____ Date_____

Center_____ Date_____

Center_____ Date_____

This sheet allows you to write children's names in the appropriate boxes as you observe the Centers. Obviously, you will need multiple copies of each of these, as you use them over an extended period of time, so you'll want to make a few blank copies, write in the names of your centers, and then copy those before filling in names.

Recently, I started adding the column headings "Alone" and "Group" under the Center names on each sheet. I do this primarily at the beginning of the year, so I can identify the children who are frequently alone and then try to determine the reasons for their situation.

If you prefer to spend more time with this assessment during a given day, you can fill in the names of all the children using each Center. You can keep the sheets on a clipboard and do this once a week for several weeks.

The information from these sheets helps you determine what your children are discovering, and which children tend to choose active activities, passive activities, or both. You'll also obtain a more in-depth understanding of your children's interests, as their freedom to choose where they will work reveals what's important to them. A summary of this information can be transferred to the *Beginning Activities Checklist*, which will show you each child's choices and interests at a glance.

Sometimes, you have a child who flits from Center to Center without being able to settle into an activity. This child needs a specific assignment to complete before going on to another (assigned) activity. Once some concentration span is developed, the child can be given a choice between two activities, but you need to pay careful attention to the activities and make sure they are completed.

You may also have a child who wants to participate in a more social activity like the Block Center, but can't seem to integrate with the other kids, even after a period of time for acclimation. In this sort of situation, I might give the child a new piece of equipment such as a truck or castle blocks or a farm. I tell the child that the equipment is his for the day and he may share it with others if he wishes, but it should be returned to me when he has finished playing with it at the Center.

This technique usually brings other children to the child and gives him a sense of power, making it especially helpful to the social development of a shy child. The same approach can be used in the Family Center, when a child seems to be left out of the mainstream. A dress-up outfit, a new doll, a purse, a different carriage — anything not previously put out for play will attract other children and allow the child in charge to direct the play for a while.

Often, this experience provides enough confidence for the child to sustain play in that Center for the day. It may or may not carry over into the next day, when something else may have to be introduced. But, it gives the child a sense of social integration and helps other children get to know the child, who is usually just too shy to become part of a social group unless the group comes to him or her.

When you redo these forms mid-year and in the spring, you will see whether each child's interests and patterns have changed, and if so, when that change occurred. This can help you chart the development of each child during the course of the year, and it can be extremely useful information during meetings with parents and colleagues.

> *This can help you chart the development of each child...*

Assessing Individual Students' Development

Due to the range of children we have in our kindergarten classrooms today, there are wide variations in the patterns of development we observe and support. Yet, keeping track of when each child reaches important milestones or achieves breakthroughs is an important part of our job, because it helps us document children's progress, understand and teach them more effectively, and discuss them more accurately with colleagues and parents.

Compiling the needed information can be done quickly and easily with the *Student Development Profile* described below. You then have a reliable written record of each child's timeline on a single piece of paper, which you can refer to and update during the year, rather than trying to rely on memory or sort through masses of papers, notes, and other materials.

Guidelines for the *Student Development Profile*

This checklist helps you record when a child achieves breakthroughs or when you become aware of a child's mastery of a skill. You do not need to fill in every line on each child's profile, but when used selectively, it provides you with an overview of each child's development during the year, which can be especially helpful when discussing children's progress with their parents.

To complete the *Student Development Profile*, simply put a check mark under the appropriate month for any skill listed or any skill that you add because it's pertinent to your program. (In a few cases, you may also want to include a number or word along with the checkmark.) Be as detailed or as selective as seems appropriate when deciding which categories you fill in for each child.

Some of the listed items are social, some are cognitive, and some identify personality characteristics. Some are easily observed, while others require checking individual students' mastery of a skill. The skills listed on the sheet are important in my classroom, and my hope is that all children can perform each skill comfortably by the end of the year.

The first 11 items listed can be filled out early in the school year, based on information gathered on the *Beginning Activities Checklist*, the *Center Participa-*

Student Development Profile

Name _____

Skill	Sept.	Oct.	Nov.	Dec.	Jan.	Feb.	Mar.	April	May	June
Plays alone comfortably										
Plays in small group comfortably										
Plays in large group comfortably										
Shows kindness										
Shows empathy										
Comfortable with school routines										
Friends chosen (fill in names)										
Favorite choice at Center time										
Cuts with scissor										
Pastes neatly										
Paints appropriately										
Appropriate pencil grip										
Writes name (upper case letters)										
Writes name (lower case letters)										
Recognizes shapes										
Can form a pattern										
Can draw a pattern										
Can describe a pattern with words										
Can apply knowledge of pattern										
Can count to (fill in #)										
Recognizes numbers to 10										
Writes numbers to 10										
Answers a question										
Speaks in full sentences										
Contributes to discussions										
Participates in story telling										
Shows interest in writing										
Recognizes letters										
Can write letters										
Uses sound/symbol understanding to sound words out										
Remembers key words										
Takes risks in learning										

From *The Kindergarten Teacher's Very Own Student Assessment Guide* by Judy Keshner. Published by Modern Learning Press, PO Box 167, Rosemont, NJ 08556, 1-800-627-5867.
This page may be reproduced by the individual purchaser only for his or her own use.

tion Form, and the *Lesson Assessment Form*, as well as your other observations of behavior.

The next 11 items deal with cognitive skills that I teach, and then note when the children master or show comfort with the skills. For instance, the four items dealing with patterns are sequential, going from concrete to representational to abstract to making connections and applying the knowledge that was internalized. My objective is to have most, if not all, of the children able to draw and describe patterns by the end of the year.

The last 10 items deal with whole language, reading readiness, use and understanding of language, and willingness to "stretch" to learn more. I hope that the children will have achieved some level of success in regard to these items by June.

We have also included a *Student Development Profile* listing the months but not the skills or characteristics, so that you can create your own list or change some of mine if you want to.

The *Student Development Profile* is a positive evaluation tool which shows only when something has been accomplished or demonstrated. It provides documentation of the skills and dispositions that children bring with them when they start school, and those that are acquired during the school year. When you review one child's Profile, you can see that child's pattern of development over time. And, when you review several Profiles together, the similarities and differences between the children are quickly and easily recognizable.

> *...you can see that child's pattern of development over time.*

Most children fall into the middle range in regard to their development, and while you need to monitor and help them conscientiously during the year, they require less thought and intervention than the children at the extremes — those who seem very bright and those who seem very young.

Very bright children require more of the materials and information you normally provide, and often they require it sooner than most other children. However, some children who initially seem very bright may simply have been trained and pushed by their parents, so their initial skills and accomplishments are far ahead of their classmates', but they lack the initiative and desire to keep moving ahead. The children who truly are highly intelligent and creative have a "spark" that keeps them growing and learning at a fast rate.

Student Development Profile

Name _____

Skill	Sept.	Oct.	Nov.	Dec.	Jan.	Feb.	Mar.	April	May	June

From *The Kindergarten Teacher's Very Own Student Assessment Guide* by Judy Keshner. Published by Modern Learning Press, PO Box 167, Rosemont, NJ 08556, 1-800-627-5867.

Whatever their cognitive abilities, we must pay careful attention to the social skills of children who seem very bright. Some children are very successful socially and academically and become natural leaders, which is a wonderful situation. Other children who lack the social skills they need may become unhappy and uncomfortable in school, which can undermine their academic careers as well as other aspects of their lives. In addition to our own efforts, we need to enlist their parents' help in supporting the social development of such children.

At the other end of the scale are the children who seem very young, many of whom may also be highly intelligent. These "late bloomers" often need more time to develop in order to succeed socially and academically, but in many schools the refusal to provide extra-time options — including retention — in the early grades drastically limits our ability to help these children.

> *These "late bloomers" often need more time to develop...*

Often, very young children are uncomfortable in kindergarten, because they cannot do what many other children do easily. This scares them and makes them want to stay away, because they know on some level that they really don't belong there. Rather than wanting to come to school even when they are sick, these sorts of children often invent illnesses so they don't have to come to school. And, when they are in the classroom, they tend to stay close to the teacher and require lots of direction, praise, and encouragement.

With or without extra-time options, we have to be ready to intervene and help these children, but not hover or stifle them. For the first few months or even longer, we need to help them develop the social skills that will enable them to feel comfortable in school. Then, we can start to introduce more cognitive material, knowing that many of these children will in fact succeed academically if allowed to proceed at their own rate, but that pressure to do too much too soon will create stress and low self-esteem that can have devastating long-term effects.

I strongly believe that children's well-being is far more important than learning any particular aspect of the curriculum at a specific time. We need to monitor each child's progress over time, without allowing the academic time frame to take precedence over children's individual rate of development.

Assessing Social Characteristics & Development

Traditionally, kindergarten has been the time and place children make the transition from the family-centered home environment to the social setting in which they must function during their elementary and high school years. While many children now have years of daycare and preschool experience when they enter our classrooms, most still engaged in parallel play during daycare and pre-school, so kindergarten remains the point at which their growing social awareness combines with group learning in a new and important way. And, for other children, kindergarten is still the first sustained encounter with any kind of group learning in a school setting.

Today, as in the past, assessing children's social characteristics and helping them with their social development is a vitally important aspect of the kindergarten teacher's job. However, the increasingly busy (and often academic) nature of today's kindergartens leaves less time to focus on children's social development. At the same time, the increased focus on academics in first grade and above results in kindergarten being the last chance for many children to work closely with a teacher on skills they will need in order to thrive in a group learning environment.

That's why we kindergarten teachers need to assess our students' social characteristics early in the year, and then continue to assess their social development throughout the year. Not only does the information we compile help us help the children to grow socially, it also helps us help them to learn and grow in other ways, as well.

The following sections of this chapter explain how to work with two checklists I developed to assess social characteristics and development. Using them to gather the information you need and respond effectively can have a profound influence on patterns of behavior which often have a long-term impact on children's lives.

Guidelines for the *Social Characteristics Checklist*

An assessment of each child's social characteristics can help you identify a variety of strengths or areas of concerns. This is observational and not difficult to do. Spending a few days early in the year watching the social Centers will enable you to see which children gravitate toward these areas. You then can observe which children are socially adept and seem to be accepted by others, and which children are socially inept and need to develop social skills in order to make their play acceptable.

I recently created the *Social Characteristics Checklist* to help me identify each child's social style or pattern of behavior. I was pleased with the results, especially because this information helped me both to understand the choices children were making at Center time and to intervene effectively where necessary.

Following is a summary of the categories listed on the checklist, with some brief comments about how I identify them and distinguish between them:

Loners do not interact with other children — even those working right nearby. Loners exist in every class at the beginning of the school year, but in my experience, only one boy remained a loner throughout the year, although he did play with a few other boys occasionally, if they played with something he wanted to be involved with at that time. This boy truly "marched to the beat of a different drummer" and continued to do so in each class he was in.

Almost all other loners stop being loners when they find a friend or acclimate to the environment, so this is usually not a long-term problem, especially if the teacher helps the loners find friends and acclimate.

Quiet children usually remain quiet, but they can be and often are social in their quiet way. These children usually have a certain demeanor which makes you aware that they are comfortable with themselves — they're self-confident, know what they want to do, and do just that. They're simply not outgoing or talkative or in need of playing with lots of other kids, although their abilities and sense of self make other children look up to them and seek their company.

Shy children, with help, become more comfortable as time goes on and enjoy other children and activities. However, they usually revert back to their shy demeanor when new situations arise — especially at the beginning of each new school year. The shy child longs for what he or she is afraid to reach for — positive interaction with other kids.

> *This is observational and not difficult to do.*

Social Characteristics Checklist

Name	Loner	Quiet	Shy	Social Skills Needs Social	Socially Adept	Other/Comments

It's definitely
worth the work.

Shy children need help in order to realize their worth — their value to themselves, you, and the rest of the class. They need to be celebrated for their work, their good ideas, their kindness, etc. This should all be casually mentioned to the class, because being at center stage embarrasses shy children. A whisper in his or her ear, or a special citation sent home, also help. And, once shy children make a friend, they are on their way. Little by little, they will feel comfortable in a group and their personality will emerge, and eventually you will see a child in love with the world you have helped him or her find. It's definitely worth the work.

Social children are focused on other kids, want to interact, and do so. They are not withdrawn and do not play alone. However, some social children interact successfully and some do not, which is why the *Social Characteristics Checklist* also has columns where you should note whether these children need social skills or are socially adept. It would be incomplete to put a check mark under social and not fill in one of the two following columns.

The *Social Characteristics Checklist* is simple to fill out, but in some cases it will require careful thought to decide where to put the check mark for a particular child. While observing a few children at a time, I keep the traits listed above in mind, and as something about a child stands out, I record it on the checklist.

Differentiating between quiet children, shy children, and loners can be particularly difficult, but it's important to do because of the different techniques needed to handle each type of child. For example, I had a very quiet little girl several years ago who I initially thought was timid and withdrawn. Day after day, all she chose to do was painting or drawing, and although she was quite proficient as an artist, she just put her work in the basket and never showed anything to me. When I returned her work and admired it aloud, she would just smile and accept my comments.

One day, when I was reading a story to the class, I noticed that she was silently reading along with me. I then talked with her mother, who told me the girl had taught herself to read at age 3, loved to draw and write stories, was the oldest of 3 sisters, and was most content by herself, doing her own thing. As the year progressed, others asked for her help at times, and she was always gracious and willing, but never did the seeking. So, I did not attempt to intervene, and

I did not worry about her. By the end of the year, she had become friends with a group of girls and began making play dates.

One ESL student I had was a loner for several months, until his understanding of and ability to speak English improved. Then, when he felt more comfortable with our language, he became a very social creature and displayed a most delightful sense of humor. By the end of the year, he was one of the more popular children, and almost a terror in his zeal for active play! So, the check mark in the Loner column at the beginning of the year moved over to the Social and Socially Adept columns when I did the checklist again later in the year. He had a happy and successful kindergarten experience, even though there were cognitive and language problems, and his good self-esteem and social skills helped him in first grade, when he was having academic difficulty.

This checklist leads into the form described in the following section, the *Class Social & Emotional Profile*, which summarizes areas of strength and concern, and provides room for your comments. Suggestions for transferring information to that form can be found in that section.

Guidelines for the *Class Social & Emotional Profile*

You don't need to list every child on the *Class Social & Emotional Profile*. Instead, its purpose is to help you assess the children at either end of the social spectrum: those who tend to be social leaders and those who tend to have trouble fitting into the group. If a child fits in well with the group but is not a leader, he or she does not really require any special attention in this area and does not need to be listed on this form.

In regard to the leaders, there are usually two different types that emerge early in the year. Natural leaders interact well with a variety of other children and stay popular all year long. These children often help the teacher and other children, in part by serving as good role models for other kids. Sometimes, I ask natural leaders to take other children "under their wing" for specific purposes.

In contrast, some children act more like "bosses," which results in other children following their lead initially, but then rebelling once they realize that their own interests and inclinations are not being respected. The "bosses" need help in developing the empathy, inclinations, and social skills that will enable them to take turns and even enjoy doing what other children want to do, at least some of the time.

...some children act more like "bosses,"...

At the other end of the spectrum are the children who do not succeed in leading or in finding a place in the group. Children in this category include the overly aggressive ones who hit other children or take their toys, and the overly withdrawn children who have difficulty making friends. An important distinction here is that shy children, as well as quiet but assured children, may make only one or two friends, and that is enough for them. When a child does not make any friends, however, or when a child frequently seeks out social contact but cannot sustain or conclude it successfully, then some assistance is warranted.

The *Class Social & Emotional Profile* can be completed once every few months, as this sort of schedule will help you identify initial social problems, monitor children's progress, and document any new problems that may develop during the school year.

Most of your observations for the *Class Social & Emotional Profile* will be made during Center time, but you should also consider children's ability to work on projects alone, in a small group, and in a large group. Other important considerations include a child's leadership ability, empathy, popularity, emotional needs, listening skills, and attention span.

Strengths or weaknesses in these areas should be noted on the form, along with any relevant comments. This information will then provide the basis for additional work with children who need to improve their social skills.

You'll also want to use information from the *Social Characteristics Checklist.* For example, if you've put a check mark in the Needs Social Skills column on the checklist, you put a corresponding note in the Area of Concern column on the *Class Social & Emotional Profile*, perhaps along with a reminder in the Comments column about a specific incident that caused concern. The same procedure can be followed with areas of strength, so you have notes and anecdotal records that are likely to reveal progress over time when you complete this form again later in the year.

For example, you might have a shy child who has not made close friends, and who avoids the Block and Family Centers because so much social interaction occurs there. If you invite the child to have tea with you in the Family Center, other children will want to join in, and this can lead to important new relationships, as well as greater self-confidence.

Or, you might have a young, exuberant child who just loves other kids and must touch, hug, kiss, take a toy, etc. This sort of child is often extremely physi-

> *...this can lead to important new relationships...*

Class Social and Emotional Profile

Date _____

Name	Areas of Strength	Areas of Concern	Comments

From *The Kindergarten Teacher's Very Own Student Assessment Guide* by Judy Keshner. Published by Modern Learning Press, PO Box 167, Rosemont, NJ 08556, 1-800-627-5867. This page may be reproduced by the individual purchaser only for his or her own use.

cal in his outgoing behavior, but he or she can be taught to tone down the touching and taking. These children need to learn to get attention by asking for what they want or touching gently, rather than grabbing or giving bear hugs. A code word — secret between you and the child — might be a way to diffuse situations, once you have instilled this "clue" in the child's memory. Discussed quietly with the understanding that this will help the child make friends and have more fun, most children who have not yet learned these social skills will cooperate.

On the other hand, the overly aggressive child who is a bully and doesn't care who he hurts — as long as he gets his way — needs a different approach. Separation from his chosen activity immediately and consistently through a short time-out (no more than 5 minutes), along with "We play safely here," or "That was not safe behavior," will produce a change in behavior after a while. As long as the teacher is firm, consistent, and doesn't lose her cool, the child will realize that he's not going to win with her on his own terms, and that every time his behavior is out-of-bounds he's being deprived of the activity he wants to be involved with. The teacher's patience and persistence are required, but the end result is a win-win situation.

> *...the end result is a win-win situation.*

By carefully watching children and compiling specific observations, you can identify social strengths and weaknesses, and usually respond effectively. After intervention, you will probably see a change the next time you watch for a situation or behavior that caused concern.

However, if I am seriously concerned about a child's social skills, I also try to involve our school social worker early in the year. I always inform parents when I do this, and the social worker calls them directly. She talks with the child individually and sometimes makes recommendations to the parents. She also has group lessons that she can use to address a particular concern I have about a child, thus involving the whole class in thinking through "what if" situations. This sometimes solves a problem, as it is a general discussion that does not focus on any particular child.

Lesson Assessment

The word "lesson" can have different meanings for kindergarten teachers. While some teachers use formal instruction to teach content or skills during the kindergarten year, this is not the approach I take. I prefer to let my students learn by doing, and the lessons I teach are really introductions to the use of new materials.

Whenever something new becomes available in the classroom, I provide a group lesson which primarily consists of directions for using the new material. I then need to determine whether the children can follow the directions and work with the material successfully. Those who cannot or do not achieve these objectives essentially become a small group, and I then review the instructions with these children and/or demonstrate the techniques they need to learn.

As explained elsewhere in this book, I do encourage and support the learning of content and skills, especially during the second half of the school year. And, of course, this sort of learning cannot always be accomplished through the use of "concrete" manipulatives. However, during the kindergarten year in particular, children need to be able to proceed at their own rate and in a developmentally appropriate way, as they make the transition to working with abstract symbols such as letters and numbers.

In the past, I did use formal instruction and worksheets to teach content and skills, but I found that creating an environment which encourages children's natural inclination to learn is more effective. Now, I only provide worksheets for use as "homework," if at all. This use of worksheets can provide reinforcement of the learning that takes place in the classroom, and many parents love it.

Whatever your approach to lessons, I believe you will find the *Lesson Assessment Form* helps you evaluate your students' achievements and your instructional methods.

Guidelines for the *Lesson Assessment Form*

This is the easiest and most versatile of all the forms and checklists I created. Whenever you have a particular objective that you are forming a lesson around, use this form to compile information about each child's response to the lesson, and his or her success at achieving the objective.

...you will also be able to evaluate the class as a whole...

Then, not only will you have information about each child's performance, you will also be able to evaluate the class as a whole in regard to the specific objective within the lesson. And, you will have the information you need when considering the effectiveness of your approach.

This form fits any group lesson or activity. It can be used for a lesson about the use of basic materials at the beginning of the year, such as handling scissors, or it can be used in regard to a more academic lesson later in the year, such as mathematical patterning activities.

One way I use this form is to assess children's Journal Writing, an activity described in more detail in the Language Arts chapter. When I want to evaluate children's progress, I walk around with a *Lesson Assessment Form* on my clipboard while they are working with their journals. I make notations as to what is written — scribbles, letters, words — and if a crayon or pencil is being used. I also note whether the finished work is shared or kept private.

I repeat this assessment late in the year to see if there's a change in the content or sharing of the journals. Some children never go beyond drawing or "scribble writing;" others switch from isolated letters to words without vowels to sentences. Some copy their Key Words, friends' names, or words from the morning story. Some children start showing other children their journals late in the year, and some never share, which is a personal choice and fine with me.

I record the information about content and sharing because it helps me understand what stage children have reached and how they are progressing. However, when I evaluate them using the symbols described below, I do so based on their ability to achieve the objective for this activity, which I would describe as "developing an interest in daily writing or drawing as a personally meaningful activity." In this respect, a child who copies or even writes words in a journal just because he or she is "supposed to" has not achieved the objective, while a child who can only draw but does so with real enthusiasm and commitment is succeeding.

To use this form with your lessons, get ready at the beginning of the year by making one copy, on which you write the names of the children down the left side, and then make numerous copies of this sheet. Make sure to save this master copy, because you'll probably use this sheet again and again during the year.

Lesson Assessment Form

Date _____   Lesson _____

Objective _____

Class Names	Assessment and Comments

When completing the *Lesson Assessment Form*, I use the same simple notations explained elsewhere in the book to record my assessment of each child's performance:

✓   learned and performed well

?   I'm not sure

X   is not accomplishing the objective

> ...*you will quickly and easily see the different levels of success...*

When you review these marks, along with any comments accompanying them, you will quickly and easily see the different levels of success achieved by the children. You will then know which children can move on to new lessons, and which ones need to do more work in order to achieve the objective of the lesson.

Language Arts Assessment

In a kindergarten classroom that is truly "developmentally appropriate," all curriculum areas are integrated and inter-related, usually through the use of a theme. (For a complete guide to an integrated kindergarten curriculum, see *Positively Kindergarten,* by Beth Lamb and Phyllis Logsdon, which is listed on the Resource page) Yet, we still need to assess children in regard to specific content areas, in order to identify individual needs and respond appropriately. Looking only at the "big picture" — rather than the many individual strengths and weaknesses which together comprise the "whole child" — does not respect the complexity and variability of children and of our responsibilities as kindergarten teachers.

This is particularly true in regard to the subject areas now known as "language arts," which at the kindergarten level include reading readiness, writing, speaking, and listening, as well as thinking. One child may be verbally precocious but have trouble listening and following directions; another child may be an enthusiastic scribbler but show little or no interest in learning to read; and so on. Identifying these different levels of interest and ability — and then providing appropriate instruction — are critical aspects of the kindergarten teacher's job, because assessment of language development is considered far more important in kindergarten than monitoring progress in subject areas such as science or social studies.

An equally important consideration is that "authentic" assessments grow directly out of children's daily classroom activities. The assessments in this book evolved along with the curriculum I used in my classroom over many years, so an understanding of my approach is needed to fully understand the assessments themselves. You'll also find information in this chapter about assessment techniques I've developed which are not directly linked to the assessment forms in this book, but which are still vital components of the assessment process.

While I believe the language arts curriculum I've used is very similar to that used by many kindergarten teachers, I also recognize that other teachers may have different preferences and requirements. I've therefore also included some thoughts at the end of this chapter about how teachers can adapt these assessments to a different teaching style and curriculum.

Specific teaching strategies and assessments

1. The Alphabet

Teaching Strategy - In my classroom, I still teach the alphabet as a "separate entity," as well as in the context of various other learning activities. Beginning in December and continuing through June, I introduce one alphabet letter per week, proceeding in alphabetical order. The letter is presented at the beginning of the week, and that night children cut out or draw pictures related to the sound of that letter. They bring the pictures to school the next day, and together we "read" them aloud. All week, we hear and recognize words which contain that sound, and at the end of the week we draw a picture for that letter in our *Alphabet Books.*

> *...we draw a picture for that letter in our* Alphabet Books.

In creating the pages of these books, the children learn to begin at the top left-hand corner of the page. I teach them to put their finger there each time, and then when I draw both upper-case and lower-case versions of the letter on the chalkboard, the children copy them into that corner of the page. We brainstorm words we've learned that have the same sound we're working on, and in the center of the page each child draws a picture related to one of the words. The children tell me what their pictures are, and I write the appropriate word at the bottom of the page, underlining the letter we're working on (see illustration below). After a while, the children start writing the words themselves.

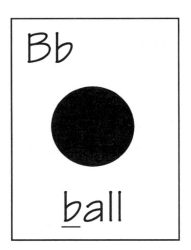

I collect all the pages and keep them in the children's language portfolios. In June, the children make their own cover pages (see next illustration), and then I staple all the pages together and let each of the children take home their own *Alphabet Book*.

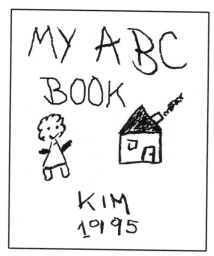

In addition, I put an illustrated alphabet card for the letter *A* on the bulletin board during the first week, and add a new card for the next letter during each of the weeks that follow. This is my ongoing visual guide for the children. When they need to know the shape of a letter they have not yet mastered, they can find it in this display by the picture clue accompanying the letter on the card.

Some other teachers go through the alphabet in different ways and avoid proceeding in alphabetical order. I follow the Alphabet Song, because I've found this approach is easier for the children who have difficulty with this level of formal work. They can always sing the song and know which letter comes next. This approach also makes it easier for parents to keep track of where we are, in order to help with the "homework." And, going in sequential order seems more logical for children who are developing cognitive awareness.

This is the only "formal" teaching of letter recognition I do. Many years ago, I also used an alphabet workbook which was not appropriate for kindergarten children, but I have since replaced it with many other hands-on activities, of which Writer's Workshop is the most important (see page 72).

To support the learning of the alphabet, I put out a variety of other materials when we have completed half the letters. The "Alpha Worm" upper and lower case manipulatives go on the toy shelf, as do the upper and lower case rubber

> *This is the only "formal" teaching of letter recognition…*

letters for tracing and puzzle use. I also put out alphabet blocks, Sesame Street alphabet cards, a picture dictionary, and lots of paper and pencils for writing. Of course, there are many manipulatives that can be made or bought which are also appropriate learning tools for kindergarten students.

Assessment - Using a chart of letters out of alphabetical order (see next page,) I point to a letter and ask the child to name it. I record all those recognized, and I also ask the child to find certain letters, which I record, as well. This is done several times during the year.

> *...I point to a letter and ask the child to name it.*

This simple assessment serves two purposes. Asking the child to identify letters I point to assesses his or her knowledge of the names of letters, and asking the child to find certain letters assesses his or her ability to recognize letters. Some children can do both, some can do one but not the other, and some children can do neither.

This information is important because many children know letters in the context of the Alphabet Song, but when the letters are presented in the scrambled format used on the chart, the real extent of their knowledge quickly becomes apparent. As kindergarten teachers, we need to know where children are on the path to literacy, and what work needs to be done to help them on their way.

A young child, such as my four-and-a-half year-old grandson, can sing the Alphabet Song, but when shown the chart can only recognize a few letters which are in his name. He also calls letters "numbers," which many young children do until they are ready to make sense of these abstract symbols.

Using formal instruction to teach letter recognition to children such as this, who are not developmentally ready, is a virtually impossible task. Instead, keep offering opportunities to see printed materials, and to "write" text for pictures. One day, when ready, each child will "bloom," be it this year or next. (I am not referring to children with a learning disability, who will need help from a specialist. This is about young children who will one day mature into cognitive awareness.)

P X Y

O N I

U B C V

H A T W

E L F J

S D Q G

K Z M R

2. Daily Story

Teaching Strategy - From October through June, we have a daily "story" on the chalkboard. I write it with the children watching, read it aloud, and then the children "read" it with me. It goes like this:

> Good (morning or afternoon). Today is (Day), (Month) (Date), (Year).
> It is a (sunny, cloudy, rainy, or snowy) day.
> Today we will go to (gym, music, library, etc.).
> Today is (a birthday, special event, missing tooth day, new brother or sister day, etc.)

From October through December, I also pick a letter, write it on the board, and call on one of the children to find that letter in one part of the story and underline it. The child then picks another child, who finds the letter in a different part of the story and underlines it. A boy picks a girl and a girl picks a boy, so that we always alternate, just as we do in the seating arrangement for our Sharing Circle.

(Initially, I used this sort of "A-B-A-B" seating arrangement because I found the children attended better and did less talking among themselves. Then, I realized from my work with *Math Their Way* that this sort of arrangement could be used to teach children about patterns, which are the foundation on which mathematical concepts are built. Patterning lessons can also contribute to language arts lessons, as when we begin to look for patterns around us — the American flag, clothing designs, tiles on the floor, etc. — and use them to develop the children's descriptive vocabulary — big, small, thick, thin, etc.

Alternating is fairer and helps more children...

This same A-B-A-B pattern is helpful when children pick each other, because it helps keep the same friends from being picked each time and monopolizing the activity. Alternating is fairer and helps more children become involved. I do try to have enough words in the story so that each child has a turn, but this isn't always possible due to time restraints and large class sizes.)

In December, when we start counting the days to the holidays and using holiday words, I change the underlining from individual letters to whole words. It takes a while for the children to adjust to this, but the rhythm and pattern begin to make sense after a week or so. We continue this activity throughout the remainder of the year.

Assessment - As you proceed with this activity, it becomes easy to discern how each child is progressing. Some children can consistently find the right

Word Recognition Form

Date _____

Knows Words	Needs Clues	No Understanding

word with ease; they either recognize the words, know where the words fit in the sequence, or recognize the beginning sound of each word. Other children need clues — the sound, the letter beginning the word, the placement of the word in the sentence, or the row the word is in. If all else fails, I write the first letter or the whole word on the board, and ask the child to match it.

I record every child's current stage each month. It takes a few days until all the children have a couple of turns, and during this time I take notes on the *Word Recognition Form* (see preceding page), which is divided into three columns. I put each child's name with a brief comment in the appropriate column, as shown below, and then transfer the information to a *Lesson Assessment Form* when time permits.

> *I record every child's current stage each month.*

Knows Words	Needs Clues	No Understanding
Allen - anywhere in story	James - begins with *d*	Robby - no letter or position recognition
	Marc - first row	
	Jean - capital letter beginning sentence	

When a child shows no recognition or a very limited understanding of letters, I ask an aide or volunteer to work with the child, or I work with the child myself, using the manipulatives, clay, crayons, and paper. We often try to focus on family names as a starting point for recognition, and I ask the parents to help at home, too.

Sometimes, a child is developmentally young or delayed, and has no interest in this work, yet. I hope that the exposure will help develop interest, but I don't burden such children with tasks that might create a pattern of resistance or avoidance, which can last a long time. These sorts of children need continued, positive exposure to stories and other forms of language, until they are ready for more focused and intensive work.

3. Writer's Workshop

Teaching Strategy - This is the best way to develop an understanding of print and the importance of letters. My school has been involved with the "writing process" for several years now, and we have found that it enables children to experience writing as a natural and pleasurable activity, rather than a scary, "must-be-perfect" lesson.

Helping kindergarten children start to write is not a complicated task. In the later grades, there is editing, first and second drafts, conferencing, etc. In kindergarten, we have a round table we call the "Writer's Table," and a chair we call the "Author's Chair." Parents from my school district are trained to work with children on their writing, which allows me to have writing as a choice during Center time whenever a volunteer comes, which often is several times per week.

Each writer takes a piece of paper (we use photocopy paper) and uses a pencil to write his or her name in the top left-hand corner, then boxes it in as shown below. The adult uses a pencil to create a separate "helper paper," by drawing a scalloped edge within the sides of the sheet, as is also shown below. The area within the scalloped edge is where letters are written to help a child who doesn't know which letter is needed. Other children can also write needed letters, as well as adults.

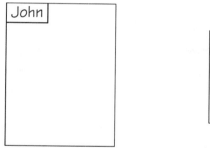

The adult asks the child what he or she would like to write about. The children usually have ideas, but sometimes they need suggestions, which can be arrived at by questioning the child about his or her interests. Once a topic is decided upon, the child states the sentence to be written, and the adult slowly sounds it out — sound-by-sound, word-by-word — while the child writes what he or she hears.

Some of the guidelines we have developed are that we don't make minor spelling corrections like *s* for *c* or *j* for *g*, and we don't add unheard sounds. No one writes on the author's paper but the author, and after the writing is finished, the author can illustrate it. Only three children can work at the Writing Center at one time, but others may come as space becomes available.

> *No one writes on the author's paper but the author...*

This process generates a wide range of results, from "scribble writing" (which I introduce to the whole class before the Writer's Workshop begins) to perfectly formed sentences, with many variations in between. Most of the writing contains "inventive" spelling and grows easier to read as the year progresses. Overall, children who are not yet fluent in letter recognition tend to learn more from this activity than other activities involving the alphabet, perhaps because this activity promotes visual, auditory, and tactile/kinesthetic involvement all at the same time.

When Center time ends and we have cleaned up, we gather around our Author's Chair. (I recently purchased a new one, which looks like a director's chair but is bright red and has "Author" printed on it. It is only used to read stories from the Writing Table, and because the kids love sitting in it, it encourages some of the more reluctant ones to write stories and read them aloud.) The adult calls each author in turn to sit in the chair, where the child "reads" his story and holds it up for everyone to see. We all applaud, and sometimes we also ask questions or make comments. In every case, time spent in the Author's Chair is a special celebration of writing and the writer.

> *...writing begins to extend into other activities.*

One outcome of this process is that writing begins to extend into other activities. The children begin to write their own inventive spelling words on their alphabet pages; they write on their drawings; they make books either alone or in cooperative groups and then want to read them to the class; they take paper and pencils into the Block and Family Centers; they write messages, cards, and letters to each other; and they write in their journals.

Writer's Workshop is a wonderful learning experience, and the process and end result work well with portfolio assessment. For more information, see Donald Graves' and Lucy Calkins' books on the writing process, some of which are listed on the Resource page.

Assessment - As you observe the children writing, you can identify the different stages that children have reached:

> who knows how to write words without help or can sound out the words;
> who can write what a helper sounds out, connecting sounds to symbols;
> who can write the letter but doesn't connect the sound;
> who needs letters written on the helper paper;
> and who cannot form letters even with the help of a sample.

You will also see which children know the letters of the alphabet out of order, and who is willing to take the risk of trying this activity.

Each child's writings are dated and filed in his or her individual writing folder, providing a chronological collection of work which can be assessed and then sent home at the end of the year, except for one or two samples which are sent on to next year's teacher. This continues right through sixth grade.

4. Journals

Teaching Strategy - In February, I give each child a notebook containing unlined pages and ask the children to write their names on the cover. I explain what a journal is — a personal book in which a page is used each day for drawing and writing. I also explain that it can be shown to others or kept private. I tell them about grown-ups' diaries and journals, and I suggest that they might always want to keep a journal.

The children write or draw on one page of their journals when they arrive each day — right after hanging up their coats and giving me notes, and before attendance is taken. Then, the journals are put in the cubbies until the next day.

Words appear in them more frequently as the year progresses, but some children only draw in theirs. Parents have an opportunity to view them in this way during Exhibit Night in May, and then the journals go home to stay in June.

Assessment - The journals are not assessed in a formal way, but looking at them toward the end of the year shows the progress that has been made in drawing and writing skills.

5. Key Word Vocabulary

Teaching Strategy - In March, I begin developing the children's individual sight word collections, called Key Words. I adapted this from the concept Sylvia Ashton-Warner describes in her book, *Teacher*, which I believe should be required reading for every teacher in grades pre-k through first.

All the children receive their own 6" x 9" brown envelopes, which they write their names on. Every day from then on, each child picks a word that he or she would like to read, and I write the word on a strip of oak tag (approximately 1" x 6"). After the child looks at the word, it is put into the envelope.

The next day, the child tries to read the word in the envelope, and then asks to have another word written. Any word that is not remembered is thrown away, because it is unimportant. But, it's amazing how many of these individually chosen words are remembered, and how quickly the collection of sight words

> *...it's amazing how many... words are remembered...*

grows. Only a child who is very young or totally disinterested in academics does not go beyond a few words by the end of year. Even children with learning problems usually remember their words.

As the collections grow, it becomes very time-consuming to do this with each child every day. So, I do it first thing in the morning and enlist the sixth-grade monitors, parents, and aides to help. If I have no help, I call a few children at a time during Center time, and listen to them then.

As the days go by, you can see the "light bulb" go on in one child after another, as each one realizes that he or she is actually *reading*. It gives children such confidence, even those who master only a few words.

By late spring, many of the children read to each other, and they are very honest about words they don't remember! Some children end up reading the words of everyone around them, as well as their own.

Assessment - After a month or two, you can clearly see the development of each child in regard to reading. The class seems to fall into groups, almost as it would if you were dividing your class into assigned reading groups based on ability.

Some children seem to learn effortlessly and know exactly what new word they want each day. They are the ones who like to read the words of everyone else at the table, as well as their own. Many of these children even learn to spell their words as they choose to copy them into their journals. They connect the discrete parts of the reading-writing process and turn into readers by the end of the year.

Other children learn their first few words and then remember some new ones, forgetting others which get discarded. These children can't always come up with a new word each day; they need time to think about it. They may have a limited vocabulary and copy another child's word, forgetting it the next day because it has no real significance for them. These children have not yet connected the different parts of the reading-writing process and so are learning isolated words, sometimes just guessing at what a word is. After learning more alphabet letters and sounds, they may begin to sound out one of their words, which enables them to remember it.

Some children seem to learn effortlessly...

By the end of the year, children for whom the entire process has no meaning will still learn a few words that matter to them. And, while these children will not have experienced the thrill of learning to read that the Key Word vocabulary offers, they will still feel successful in regard to the words they have learned. These children need time to grow, and the initial feeling of success will help sustain and motivate them before and after they are ready to learn to read.

If you listen to several children each day reading their Key Words during the spring, while you jot down what each child is doing on a *Lesson Assessment Form*, you will have important information needed for your *Year-End Assessment Summary*. And, you will really see how much they all have developed and learned since starting their Key Words.

6. Class Books

Teaching Strategy - All year, we write class books that go into our classroom library. Beginning with *What I Like Best About School*, created at the end of the first week of school, and continuing through all the holidays and seasons, we create feelings books, food books, "snow day" books, etc., until we create an updated version of *What I Like Best About School* during the last week of the school year.

Using 9" x 12" manila drawing paper, each child draws a picture about our topic and then tells me what to write under the picture. (Once the Writer's Table has been in operation for a while, some of the children begin to write their story words themselves.) I fasten all the pages together with a colored-paper cover and write an appropriate title on it. As soon as it's complete, I read the book to the class, and we applaud all the authors and illustrators.

Assessment - At the end of the year, I undo all the books and assemble each child's pages. I do this in the order in which the books were created, and by looking through the pages, I see the growth and development that took place from the fall through the spring. Along with the growth in writing skills, the pictures show growth in fine-motor coordination, use of detail, complexity of form, spatial relationships, and overall level of maturity. After reviewing the pages, I send them home in a folder with a note for parents.

> *I see the growth and development that took place...*

7. Class Library and Listening Center

Teaching Strategy - Many of the books I read to the children have tapes that go along with them. In particular, all of the "big books" have accompanying small books and tapes. After reading a book aloud, I put it in the Listening Center, or classroom library, or both. (All of the big books go into the library.)

The children have opportunities to read and/or listen to the books every day. During Center time, the children go to the classroom library to look at books, and the Listening Center is also available for children who want to read and listen. Most children love to hear their favorite stories again and again, as well as new ones, so the Listening Center is one of the favorites and is utilized constantly. In addition, classroom library books are sometimes taken into the Family Center and "read" to the baby dolls. Children also "pretend" to be going to the library from the Family Center.

Other than Center time, classroom library books are used as models when children write and are used to help learn about a variety of subjects, so the books are integrated into all areas of the curriculum and used throughout the day.

Assessment - I keep notes on which children frequent the library and Listening Center, what choices each child makes, and how the children behave during their sessions. Some children prefer to lie quietly on a cushion and read; others prefer to read aloud, showing the pictures as I do. (Parents tell me this is often done at home.) In addition, I note whether my interested readers and listeners are also the writers and Key Word readers, as well as those who know the daily story words.

This is an informal, observational type of assessment, where you're looking at what children are interested in, rather than checking for specific skills and knowledge. Reviewing the *Center Participation Forms* over a period of several weeks will show you which children's names appear frequently in the space for the library and/or Listening Center. Then, you can also see whether those children's names continue to appear throughout the year, or just at specific times. And, when you fill out the *Student Development Profile*, each child's choices, preferences, and abilities become clear, and you can make correlations among the different areas of language development.

The activities in the library and Listening Center, combined with those described in the previous sections of this chapter, comprise an effective "whole language" approach to language arts instruction. And, when assessed, these activities help you obtain a clear picture of each child's language development.

> *...the Listening Center is one of the favorites...*

Your approach may differ from mine to a greater or lesser extent, but every kindergarten teacher works with language in a variety of ways throughout the year. And, every teacher has some way of noting different aspects of children's language development. As with other assessment techniques and materials described in this book, the approach I use in regard to language arts may work perfectly for you "as is," or need some modification to meet your preferences and requirements.

Either way, I'm sure you will find, as I have, that documenting and reviewing children's growth in this crucial area not only makes you a more effective teacher, it provides a great deal of satisfaction when you look back at the end of the year and see how much progress each child has made.

Assessing Mid–Year Activities

By the middle of the year, the more mature children have moved beyond constant play in the Block and Family Centers. These children are working more with art materials and cognitive manipulatives. They are writing and looking at books in the classroom library, as well as listening to tapes at the Listening Center. When they paint and draw, they want print attached to their work. These children are creating and finding patterns everywhere, not just with the math materials. They grab on to each newly introduced material, and they enjoy board games and more difficult puzzles.

The younger children continue to prefer playing in the more social areas, such as the Block and Family Centers, but their pretend play becomes more sophisticated and complex. Some younger children remain attached to the Family Center until the last day it's available in June, and then miss it terribly in first grade. Their need for this type of interaction has not yet been satiated or fulfilled.

The younger children also love the puppets and the puppet theatre, as well as my cardboard "play store." They use the math manipulatives as toys and experiment with them, but these children do not focus on specific math content, such as pattern making, until it becomes relevant to them. This happens when they are developmentally ready to see the connections linking free play to a more sophisticated interpretation.

There is no right or wrong in the differing interests and rates of learning within the class; only normal differences in developmental levels which are found in any kindergarten class.

Guidelines for the *Mid-Year Activities Checklist*

This is the second assessment of children's interests and activities during the year. The *Mid-Year Activities Checklist* includes information about the Learning Centers which were also considered when completing the *Beginning Activities Checklist*, so you may want to refer to the guidelines for that checklist to refresh your memory about those items, as that information is not repeated here.

Of course, this checklist also contains additional sections corresponding to additions to the curriculum since the beginning of the year. You'll find that the column heading "Art Activities" has replaced the individual art activities listed on the *Beginning Activities Checklist*. New columns on this checklist include "Math Materials," "Journals," "Writing Table," and "Computer." And, as on the other checklists, there are blank columns for other categories you want to include.

Following is some information about the new categories to help you complete this checklist:

Math Materials - There are various hands-on math activities that I make accessible to the children. Along with the buckets of "stuff" that I use for my *Math Their Way* program, such as geo-boards, tiles, unifix cubes, pattern blocks, "junk" boxes, etc., I also put out wooden dominoes, rubber number puzzles, number books, numerals to trace, scales, and counting games.

A child who frequently plays with math materials and/or shows an interest in numbers would have a ✓ placed by his name in the Math Materials column. If a child has inappropriate difficulty with math materials and/or shows a lack of comprehension in this area, I put an **X** by his name and a note explaining the reason in the Comments column. This child is likely to need one-on-one work, going back to the first frustration point and proceeding from there. No particular interest in the math materials requires no notation at this point.

Journals - As described in the chapter on Language Arts Assessment, every child keeps a journal during the second half of the year, but some children take more pleasure in this activity than others. Just put a ✓ next to the names of children who really enjoy writing in their journals and work diligently at it.

Writing Table - Put a ✓ in the Writing Table column for those children who often go to the table by choice. By late April or early May, you should make a list of the children who still do *not* qualify for a ✓ in this column. At that point, I begin to send them to the Writing Table during Center time, so they begin to learn the process and develop their alphabet and thinking skills.

Computer - The children in my classes are fascinated with computers and love their scheduled time in the computer lab. I also have one computer in my room, and some children just want to work there every day. Others may not show any interest or may not seem to find time for it. I put a ✓ next to the names of children who are interested in the computer and use it, noting any pertinent information in the Comments column.

> *...children in my classes are fascinated with computers...*

Mid-Year Activities
Checklist

Name	Blocks	Family Center	Art Activities	Listening Center	Puzzles	Games	Toy Manipulatives	Math Materials	Science Materials	Library	Journals	Writing Table	Computer	Comments

From The Kindergarten Teacher's Very Own Student Assessment Guide by Judy Keshner. Published by Modern Learning Press, PO Box 167, Rosemont, NJ 08556, 1-800-627-5867. This page may be reproduced by the individual purchaser only for his or her own use.

As with the *Beginning Activities Checklist*, much of the information for this checklist can be compiled by walking around the room with notepaper and the *Center Participation Forms* on a clipboard, observing children's choice of activities and participation in them. When completing the checklist, I also consider other observations I have made of children working individually and in groups.

Upon completion of the *Mid-Year Activities Checklist*, compare it with the *Beginning Activities Checklist* to see where and how each child has grown. If a child has remained "stuck" with the same choices, it may be time to suggest other activities and help the child become involved in them. However, a child constantly choosing to work in the Family Center might simply have found this delightful world relatively late and now is just beginning to explore it. Or, a child who felt shy initially may now feel comfortable there and be experiencing tremendous social growth. A review of your checklists will help you decide.

You might also want to complete the *Social Characteristics Checklist* at this time of year, or take another look at the one you completed earlier and see if your assessments during the fall still hold true. This process is usually gratifying, because most children will have opened up and acclimated socially by mid-year. Sometimes, the growth is so great that it takes your breath away!

In most cases, I don't really "do" anything about children's choice of activities, other than to monitor the choices, guide shy children into more social activities, and see that behavior is appropriate. Remembering that all children do not start kindergarten at exactly the same maturational level, I use the *Mid-Year Activities Checklist* to determine the extent of the growth and the shifting of interests demonstrated by each child, and it then becomes another important bench mark I can look back at after completing the *Spring Assessment*.

> *This process is usually very gratifying…*

Spring Assessment

By the spring, academic work has become an integral part of the curriculum. At least half of the alphabet has been taught, Journal Writing and Key Words are daily activities, and math work has progressed through patterning and into numbers. Writer's Workshop is in full swing, and the children are making individual books, cooperative books with a few friends, and class books.

While there is a greater emphasis on cognitive learning, it continues to occur in a developmentally appropriate way. Play in the Blocks and Family Centers still flourishes, although it has become more sophisticated, and floor puzzles have been added to the toy shelf selections. Drawings and paintings often contain print which the children wrote themselves. Socializing extends into the late afternoon through "play dates" and other activities.

The children have matured a lot, and this becomes evident when next year's kindergartners come to visit in May. Wherever a child was developmentally when the school year began, there is now obvious growth in a number of areas. And, the assessment form described below is designed to document the changes that have occurred, as well as each child's progress in new areas.

Guidelines for the *Spring Assessment Form*

This is an individual assessment that I do with one or two children each day, beginning in late March and continuing through April or even into May, if I have a large class. Many of the items on the *Spring Assessment Form* are exactly the same as those on the *Baseline Assessment Form* used during the previous spring or at the start of the school year, so a comparison of the two will clearly show the extent of each child's development in several important areas during the previous months.

The main difference between the *Spring Assessment Form* and the *Baseline Assessment Form* is that this form includes new items assessing children's cognitive development, as well as some other items appropriate for children who are six-years-old or will be soon. (The *Spring Assessment Worksheet*, which I use like the *Baseline Assessment Worksheet* to record my initial notes, also reflects these differences.) The information below mainly covers the new items, as the procedures for the other items are described in the section regarding Baseline Assessment (see pages 15-28).

> *...I also consider my knowledge of what occurred during the year...*

The first six items on this form are handled in the same way as they were on the *Baseline Assessment Form*. The first new question I ask children is if they are missing any teeth. When completing this item, I also consider my knowledge of what occurred during the year and what I can now see for myself, in regard to the appearance of permanent teeth as well as the loss of baby teeth. This information is an important indicator of physical development, and some educators believe it correlates with children's readiness to read and write.

The letter recognition items on the *Spring Assessment Form* are a continuation of the assessment described in the Alphabet section of the chapter on Assessing Language Arts. As explained there, asking a child to identify or find letters randomly written on a sheet helps me distinguish those children who truly know their letters from those who merely recite the Alphabet Song. For the *Spring Assessment,* I have also created a sheet (which appears on page 88) displaying randomly placed lower-case letters.

The numeral recognition item uses a similar approach with the numerals 1 through 12, clarifying which children can recognize specific numbers, and which children can only recognize numbers as part of a particular sequence they have memorized. To assess this, you can use the sheet on page 89 which has numbers written out of order on it.

For the counting item, I ask each child to count starting with the number one, and then I stop the child when he or she starts missing numbers, or reaches 100, or says, "That's all I know." If a child does not start counting when I first ask, I prompt a response by saying, "One, two, three..."

In addition to the counting, I check on mathematical ability by asking a few simple questions, such as, "If I have 2 apples and you have 2, how many do we have together?" or "If you have 5 cookies and eat 2 of them, how many do you have left?"

Without the use of props, these sorts of questions are difficult for young children, because they are abstract and require mental calculations. One or two addition questions and the same number of subtraction questions should therefore be enough to obtain the data you need, which I record as follows:

✓	can do
F	uses fingers
?	can do some but not others - inconsistent
X	cannot do

Spring Assessment Form

Name	Writes name	Draws shapes	Writes numbers 1-20	Draws a person	Knows birthday	Likes to do best	Teeth missing	Recognizes upper case letters	Recognizes lower case letters	Recognizes numerals 1-12	Counts to ____ from 1	Can do simple calculations	Answers with understanding about nursery rhyme	Comments

b f i o c

u x t v

h p a j

s k y

g n r d w

e m q l

z

11

10

7

2

5

1

8

6

4

3

9

12

To check on a child's listening and thinking skills, I ask each child to listen to a rhyme, and then I recite "Jack and Jill." (You can use any rhyme you and your children are comfortable with.) I first note whether the child just listens, or chimes in, or says, "I know that." Then, I ask a few questions such as, "What happened to Jill?" and "What's another word for 'fetch?'"

I put a ✔ next to the child's name if the child answers each question, and I write the actual words in the Comments column if they are unusual or particularly interesting. I put an **X** in the column if the child cannot answer the questions or does not seem to understand.

I might also ask whether the child knows any other nursery rhymes, and if so, I ask the child to tell them to me. We recite nursery rhymes in class throughout the school year, so this helps me assess whether there is an understanding of content, rote memory recitation, or no impact on the child at all. I like to know whether children have learned any nursery rhymes at home, too.

You may use a lot of poetry or songs in your class, and you can change this part of the assessment to something more pertinent to your program. Questions about a favorite book — including, "How would you change the ending?" — are other options for a mature child.

This is a brief look at literacy — how each child takes in this part of your language arts program. Hopefully, all the children will have assimilated some knowledge from books, poems, songs, and rhymes. You are the best judge of how to evaluate this.

There are very few kindergarten children who do not react to at least one of the literacy questions described above. When I have a child who does not react to any of them, I try to enlist the parents in reading at home, visiting the library, listening to books on tape, etc. I lend my books when such a child takes to a story, and encourage the child to share the books with his or her family. Some children come from homes which contain no books, so this is a way to introduce literature to such families.

I also encourage parents to create writing cases which have paper, pencils, markers, crayons, alphabet letters, books, tape, scissors, fasteners, etc., so that the children can draw and write their own stories, and make books. This greatly encourages interest in print.

> *You are the best judge of how to evaluate this.*

When I compare each child's *Spring Assessment* with his or her *Baseline Assessment*, I expect to see growth in every area, which I can then review with parents during the spring conferences. Some children may show little or no growth in a few areas, in which case I express my concerns about these areas to the parents. On the rare occasions when there has been little or no growth in most or all areas, I tell the parents that there is a need to take a serious look at how the child is functioning and why so little growth has occurred.

Of course, I am also careful to put each child's growth in perspective, explaining that it is based on where the child started, which may or may not be different than what the school expects. A child who seemed young when starting kindergarten may have made substantial progress, but still not have developed the level of cognitive awareness needed to succeed in first grade. So, in this sort of situation I am careful to explain where the child is now, and where the child is expected to be at the start of first grade.

I recognize that continued growth is likely to occur in the remaining spring and summer months, and that sometimes a problem is resolved because a parent finally focuses on it during the spring conference and starts taking action — or at least starts paying attention to it, which may be all that's required. However, I and many other experienced teachers have found that we often correctly identify late bloomers who would benefit from extra time, as well as children with long-lasting problems who would benefit from a special education referral.

For example, I recently had a boy who did well socially in kindergarten but clearly had a problem academically. By the time I did the *Spring Assessment*, he had only memorized about four Key Words, and he could identify about three numbers and perhaps a few more letters. He could not link letters to words, and clearly had trouble remembering and making connections. I felt a special education placement would be best for this child, but his parents did not want that and sent him on to first grade with special assistance. He was lucky to have a very gifted and caring first grade teacher, but even she was unable to help him make sufficient progress.

The boy will still probably end up in special ed, and now is likely to need additional counseling to help him cope with the frustration, fear, and sense of failure he has experienced during his first few years of school. That's why I believe it is so important for kindergarten teachers to be honest and direct with parents during the spring conferences. The parents may not accept what we have to say, but at least we will know we have done all we could for the children who are having trouble.

> *...we will know we have done all we could...*

Spring Assessment Worksheet

Name _____ Date _____ Birthdate _____

	Notation	Comments
Teeth missing		
Recognizes upper case letters		
Recognizes lower case letters		
Recognizes numerals 1-12		
Counts to ____ from 1		
Can do simple calculations		
Answers with understanding about nursery rhyme		

Year–End Assessment

We started the school year with many questions about our incoming students, and in the late spring we have many other questions to consider, as we look back at the development that has occurred and look ahead to the very important and often difficult transition to first grade. On this page and several that follow I have listed many of the questions I consider, but probably you will have additional questions you want to add to mine.

The following questions correspond to the categories on the *Year-End Assessment Summary* included in this section. You need not have all positive or all negative answers in a given area, or even answers to every question for every child. The questions give you food for thought as to what you're looking for when assessing growth, and they should help you form a final impression of each child in each specific area.

Physically, how has the child grown? Are the gross-motor and fine-motor skills age-appropriate, and have they shown signs of maturing since the fall? Has the child lost any teeth, and have any permanent teeth come in?

Socially and emotionally, how has the child grown? If initially shy and quiet, does the child now interact well with other children? Does he or she have a place within the group and feel like a valued member of it? If initially aggressive and/or overbearing, has the child learned social skills? Does he wait for his turn and listen to others? Is she a leader or a follower, and has this changed since school began? Overall, is his or her behavior indicative of a successful six-year-old? (See the Gesell Institute's *School Readiness* for behavior characteristics of five and six-year-olds. Also, Jim Grant's *"I Hate School!"* lists "Signs and signals of school stress" by age level.)

Have the concerns you noted in your anecdotal records been resolved, or have they grown worse? Does the child show empathy and consideration for others? Does he or she understand rules and why we have them? Is the child concerned with the group's well-being, and with safety? Does she seem happy and well-adjusted? Does he like school?

As you think about each child in the social-emotional context, you might want to summarize your findings in one or two sentences or a short paragraph. Then, you will be ready to fill in the *Year-End Assessment Summary*.

Most of the children will probably have exhibited relatively normal social development. For those who did not learn social skills and behavior — the ones who have not found their place in the group or who alienate other children — you need to plan an honest but sensitive conference with the parents, so that you can share both your positive assessments and your concerns.

Nothing at this conference should come as a surprise to the parents, if you have been communicating throughout the year and passing along information from your assessment forms. Be prepared with a plan to help ease the transition to the next teacher, as well as suggestions as to how the parents can work with the child during the summer.

In regard to speech and language, does the child speak clearly and express ideas in ways that are understood by others? Is he or she on target during class discussions? Does the child listen carefully, attend to the task, and focus on what is going on? Or, is the child easily distracted, and if so, has the ability to attend to a task shown some improvement since the beginning of the year? Is his use of language age-appropriate? Does she need speech intervention?

> *Be very honest in your evaluation...*

Be very honest in your evaluation of each child's speech and language, and share any concerns you have with the speech therapist for your school, as well as the child's parents. Initial problems should have shown improvement by now. Any remaining concerns need to be dealt with as soon as possible, because the evaluation process is lengthy, and weeks or months can go by before a child actually starts receiving help. When in doubt, ask for an initial evaluation. (Better safe than sorry.)

In regard to reading, does the child recognize upper and lower case letters, and can he or she label them? Does he have sound-symbol awareness? Can she read? Does he have a solid sight-word vocabulary? Is she a writer?

Does the child recognize numerals 0-12 by sight? Can he or she label them? How high can she count? Can he count backwards from 10? (My children can, because all year long at snack time we say, "10-9-8-7-6-5-4-3-2-1-0. You may begin!" This is a painless and effective way to teach counting backwards, and I would be concerned if a child had not mastered counting backwards by the end of the year.) Can the child form a pattern and "read" it? Does he recognize patterns around him?

Cognition assessment needs to be done individually with each child. As explained in the chapter on Spring Assessment, I use a variety of questions and tasks that give me answers to important questions.

Turning to some of the less specific aspects of cognition, is the child a critical thinker or a problem solver? Does he take risks when learning? Is she curious? Does he grasp new concepts easily and make connections? Does she learn by rote? Must things be repeated several times? Does the child grow upset if he or she doesn't understand something?

Does he work best alone, with one other child, in a small group, or a whole group? Is she most comfortable with teacher-directed activities, or exploring and discovering independently? Is he a concrete thinker, or has he advanced to the abstract? Is her learning style primarily visual, auditory, or tactile/kinesthetic?

Answering these sorts of questions for each child is more difficult, but attempting to do so really helps you to focus on each child, as well as to complete your *Year-End Assessment Summary.*

Overall, are you convinced that this child is ready for the environment of the next grade, and that he or she will function well there? If you are concerned that the child will have difficulty coping, do you think he or she will succeed with some help in key areas? Is the child's general level of development above average, average, or below average? Do you have the documentation to back up your answers?

Asking myself these questions about each child helps me consider each specific area of development, as well as clarify my assessment of the whole child, especially when one aspect of a child's development does not seem to fit the overall impression. I have included them here as suggestions about the information you might consider important, and you'll find that each paragraph pertains to a section on the *Year-End Assessment Summary* and can help guide you when completing this form.

Guidelines for the *Year-End Assessment Summary*

By considering the preceding questions and looking at all the assessment forms you have completed during the school year, you will see the growth that has occurred in each area, and a profile of each child should clearly emerge. You can then complete the *Year-End Assessment Summary* by filling in the following codes:

AA Above Average
A Average
BA Below Average

> *...a profile of each child should clearly emerge.*

Year-End Assessment Summary

Name	Size	Physical		Emotional		Social				Cognitive				Reading		Math			Overall Development	Comments
		Gross-motor / Fine-motor / Secure	Self-control / Self-esteem	Friendly / Aggressive / Leadership	Comfort in group / Liked by others	Speech/language / Focus/attends	Thinking skills	Concrete/abstract	Letter recognition / Sound/symbol	Reads	Number recognition	Counting	Writes numbers / Patterns							

From *The Kindergarten Teacher's Very Own Student Assessment Guide* by Judy Keshner. Published by Modern Learning Press, PO Box 167, Rosemont, NJ 08556, 1-800-627-5867. This page may be reproduced by the individual purchaser only for his or her own use.

This approach provides you with a quick overview of each child. And, especially if you highlight the **BA**'s, it is easy to spot the children who are below average in several categories and may therefore be at risk. The Comments column can be used to summarize your recommendations and concerns, which can then be reviewed by the first grade teacher along with the rest of the data on this form.

For children at either end of the spectrum — those at risk and those who excel — I created the *Year-End Special Needs Form* described below. I found that this was especially helpful at the "case conferences" where we discuss children who might be eligible for special services or placement during the following year. And, being well-prepared for these conferences has grown increasingly important, as specialists in many schools have become so busy they have little or no time for children who have not been "declared."

Guidelines for the *Year-End Special Needs Form*

This form provides a quick and easy overview of just those kids who may benefit from some sort of special assistance. It is easier for me and for other people to review than the more detailed forms and checklists, which I also bring to case conferences and refer to when asked for more information.

Children whose names appear on this form are usually doing very well or very poorly in several categories, rather than just one. Their performance may be consistent throughout, or a combination of highs and lows, such as a child who is very advanced cognitively but has emotional and behavior problems. Many other children, whose performance is consistently in the middle range, do not need to be listed on this form at all.

Following is a brief summary of the categories which appear on this form:

Speech/Language - This includes those whose speech is difficult to understand, as well as those who seem to have language processing problems. I might also include a child who continues to have difficulty pronouncing specific letters or combinations.

Emotional - The children I list in this column frequently resort to crying, refusal, and saying "I can't." I also include children who become overwhelmed in certain situations, such as a child who seems happy only during play time or gym, and then becomes long-faced and doesn't want a turn when we do academic work late in the year.

> *This approach provides you with a quick overview of each child.*

Environmental - Here I list children who still do not seem comfortable in kindergarten, even though it's a world made for children. These children often seem young and have a sense that they do not belong in kindergarten.

Social - This is the place to note the children who tend to be belligerent or withdrawn, as well as any others who cannot yet sustain socially acceptable behavior.

Perception - In addition to those children who seem have problems seeing well, I also include those who appear to have eye-hand coordination problems.

Cognitive - This is where it is especially important to list the children who excel, as well as those who are at-risk. For example, I have had a child who was reading at a third grade level by the end of kindergarten, and who benefited greatly from a special reading program set up by her first grade teacher and the librarian. I have also had a child who had no sense of patterns or numbers at the end of kindergarten, and who was still making trains in the Blocks Center while other kids were drawing up blueprints for elaborate buildings.

Behavior - The kids to be listed in this column are obvious, because they are a "pain" for virtually everyone in the class to deal with, due to frequently obnoxious and/or teasing behavior. In schools with several first grade classes, these children need to be separated so they are not all in one class.

Using the *Year-End Assessment Summary* as my primary source, I use one line on the *Year-End Special Needs Form* per child, writing the child's name under each appropriate column heading, along with one of the following codes:

E   Excels
C   Concerns
AR   At-Risk

> *...a quick look across gives you a summary of the "hot spots"...*

When the form is completed in this way, a quick look down will show you all the children doing very well or very poorly in a specific area. And, a quick look across gives you a summary of the "hot spots" for a specific child. This makes it easy for you to identify those who are clearly at-risk, as well as those who may need enrichment or an individual advanced program.

Year-End Special Needs Form

Speech/ Language	Emotional	Environmental	Social	Perception	Cognitive	Behavior

Conclusion

Teachers, not test scores, are the best evaluators of children during the kindergarten year. We obtain authentic assessments by observing children carefully, organizing who and for what purpose we observe each day, and recording our observations in a comfortable and accurate way.

This sort of assessment, along with portfolios of each child's work, reveals the whole child — his or her skills, expertise, personality, and needs — enabling us to work effectively with the children, their parents, other staff members, and administrators.

When we compile information about kindergarten children in this way, we know them best, and we can prove it!

Recommended Resources

Ames, Louise Bates and Francis Ilg. *Your Five Year Old.* New York: Dell Publishing.

Ames, Louise Bates. *Why Am I So Noisy? Why Is She So Shy?* Rosemont, NJ: Modern Learning Press.

Ashton-Warner, Sylvia. *Teacher.* New York: Bantam Books.

Baratta-Lorton, Mary. *Mathematics Their Way.* Reading, MA: Addison-Wesley.

Calkins, Lucy McCormick. *The Art of Teaching Writing.* Portsmouth, NH: Heinemann.

Clemens, Sydney Gurewitz. *The Sun's Not Broken, A Cloud's Just in the Way.* Mt. Rainier, MD: Gryphon House.

Coletta, Anthony. *Guide to Kindergarten Readiness.* Rosemont, NJ: Modern Learning Press.

Derman-Sparks, Louise and the A.B.C. Task Force. *Anti-Bias Curriculum: Tools for Empowering Young Children.* Washington, DC: National Association for the Education of Young Children.

Faber, Adele and Elaine Mazlish. *How To Talk So Kids Will Listen and Listen So Kids Will Talk.* New York: Avon Books.

Grant, Jim. *Every Parent's 5-Year-Old Owner's Manual.* Rosemont, NJ: Modern Learning Press.

Grant, Jim. *"I Hate School!"* Rosemont, NJ: Modern Learning Press.

Graves, Donald and Virginia Stuart. *Write from the Start.* New York: E.P. Dutton.

Hohmann, Mary et al. *Young Children in Action.* Ypsilanti, MI: The High Scope Press.

Ilg, Francis et al. *School Readiness.* New York: Harper & Row.

Keshner, Judy. *Starting School: A Parent's Guide to the Kindergarten Year.* Rosemont, NJ: Modern Learning Press.

Lamb, Beth and Phyllis Logsdon. *Positively Kindergarten.* Rosemont, NJ: Modern Learning Press.

Singer, Dorothy and Tracey Revenson. *A Piaget Primer: How a Child Thinks.* New York: New American Library.

Vail, Priscilla. *Learning Styles.* Rosemont, NJ: Modern Learning Press.

Other Great Publications for Kindergarten Teachers Available from Modern Learning Press

Starting School
A Parent's Guide to the Kindergarten Year
by Judy Keshner

Positively Kindergarten
A Classroom-proven, Theme-Based, Developmental Guide for the Kindergarten Teacher
by Beth Lamb & Phyllis Logsdon

"I Hate School!"
by Jim Grant

Kindergarten Readiness Guide
by Anthony Coletta, Ph.D.

Learning Styles
Food for Thought & 130 Practical Tips for Teachers K-4
by Priscilla L. Vail

**For more information
call toll-free
1-800-627-5867**